Dow   2 CDs held at desk   ESOL   428.24 CAM

D0552624

Cambridge First Certificate in English 7

WITH ANSWERS

Examination papers from University of Cambridge ESOL Examinations: English for Speakers of Other Languages

FARNHAM COLLEGE

Morley Road · Farnham · Surrey · GU9 8LU
Telephone 01252 716988   Fax 01252 723969

CAMBRIDGE
UNIVERSITY PRESS

CAMBRIDGE UNIVERSITY PRESS
Cambridge, New York, Melbourne, Madrid, Cape Town, Singapore, São Paulo

Cambridge University Press
The Edinburgh Building, Cambridge CB2 8RU, UK

www.cambridge.org
Information on this title: www.cambridge.org/9780521611596

© Cambridge University Press 2005

It is normally necessary for written permission for copying to be obtained *in advance* from a publisher. The candidate answer sheets at the back of this book are designed to be copied and distributed in class. The normal requirements are waived here and it is not necessary to write to Cambridge University Press for permission for an individual teacher to make copies for use within his or her own classroom. Only those pages which carry the wording '© UCLES 2005 Photocopiable ' may be copied.

First published 2005
6th printing 2007

Printed in the United Kingdom at the University Press, Cambridge

A catalogue record for this publication is available from the British Library

ISBN 978-0-521-61159-6 Student's Book with answers
ISBN 978-0-521-61158-9 Student's Book
ISBN 978-0-521-61163-3 Set of 2 Cassettes
ISBN 978-0-521-61162-6 Set of 2 Audio CDs
ISBN 978-0-521-61161-9 Self-study Pack

Contents

Thanks and acknowledgements

The publishers are grateful to the following for permission to use copyright material. It has not been possible to identify the sources of all the material used and in such cases the publishers would welcome information from the copyright owners.

For the extract on p. 27 from 'Treasure Island' by Brian Pendreigh, published in *The Sunday Times* on 2nd August 1998 (C) NI Syndication; for the extract on p. 28 from *American Pastoral* by Philip Roth, published by Jonathan Cape. Copyright (C) 1997 by Philip Roth. Reprinted by permission of Houghton Mifflin Company. All rights reserved. And by permission of The Random House Group Limited in the British Commonwealth; for the extract on p. 51 from 'Risk' by John Vidal, published in *The Guardian* on 9 June 1999, and for the extract on p. 57 from 'Young Shoppers' by Frances Rickford, published in *The Guardian* on 21 September 1993, and for the text on p. 78 'The Runningman', with kind permission of Alex Bellos, published in *The Guardian* on 15 October 1999 (C) Guardian; for the article on p. 42 'Bigfoot', published in the *Daily Telegraph* Young Telegraph Supplement 13 Feb 1999, and for the text on p. 75 'Memory Test' by Jerome Burne, published in the *Sunday Telegraph* 26 Oct 1997 (C) Telegraph Group Limited; for the article on p. 76 'Acting minus the drama' by Benedicte Page, published in *The Bookseller* on 23 April 1999.

Colour section

ACESTOCK.COM for pp.C14/15, C14/15; Action Images for p.C6/C7; Alamy/James Frank for p.C5 (top), Alamy/Jim Pickerell for p.C10/C11; Anthony Blake Photo Library/ Eaglemoss for p.C14/15; Corbis for p.C13 (top), Corbis/Dave Bartruff for p.C6/C7, Corbis/Richard Olivier for p.C1. (bottom), Corbis/Phil Schermeister for p.C6/C7; Getty Images/Image Bank for pp.C6/C7, C14/15, Getty Images/Lonely Planet for p.C16 (top), Getty Images /Photodisc for pp.C6/C7, C13 (bottom), Getty Images/Stone for pp.C10/C11, C16 (bottom), Getty Images/Taxi for pp.C1 (top), C6/C7; Image State for p.C5 (bottom), Image State /AGE /Fotostock for p.C4 (bottom), Image State/Premium for p.C14/15; Life File/Emma Lee for p.C14/15, Life File/Jan Suttle for p.C1O/C11; Pictures Colour Library/Clive Sawyer for p.C12 (top), Pictures Colour Library/ PhotoLocation Ltd for p.C14/15, Pictures Colour Library/Picture Finders for p.C4 (top); PowerStock/Doug Scott for pp.C10/C11, C10/C11, PowerStock/HimsI for p.C6/C7, PowerStock/Javier Larrea for p.C10/C11, PowerStock /Richard G for p.C10/C11; PowerStockJ D Dallett for p.C8 (top); Rex Features/John Harmah for p.C8 (bottom), Rex Feature/SIPA Press for pp.C12 (bottom), C9 (top), C9 (bottom).

Artwork: Oxford Designers & Illustrators

Picture research by Valerie Mulcahy

Design concept by Peter Ducker

Cover design by Dunne & Scully

The recordings which accompany this book were made at Studio AVP, London.

Introduction

This collection of four complete practice tests comprises past papers from the University of Cambridge ESOL Examinations First Certificate in English (FCE) examination; students can practise these tests on their own or with the help of a teacher.

The FCE examination is part of a group of examinations developed by Cambridge ESOL called the Cambridge Main Suite. The Main Suite consists of five examinations that have similar characteristics but are designed for different levels of English language ability. Within the five levels, FCE is at Level B2 in the *Council of Europe's Common European Framework of Reference for Languages: Learning, teaching, assessment.* It has also been accredited by the Qualifications and Curriculum Authority in the UK as a Level 1 ESOL certificate in the National Qualifications Framework. The FCE examination is widely recognised in commerce and industry and in individual university faculties and other educational institutions.

Examination	Council of Europe Framework Level	UK National Qualifications Framework Level
CPE Certificate of Proficiency in English	C2	3
CAE Certificate in Advanced English	C1	2
FCE First Certificate in English	B2	1
PET Preliminary English Test	B1	Entry 3
KET Key English Test	A2	Entry 2

Further information

The information contained in this practice book is designed to be an overview of the exam. For a full description of all of the above exams including information about task types, testing focus and preparation, please see the relevant handbooks which can be obtained from Cambridge ESOL at the address below or from the website at: www.CambridgeESOL.org

University of Cambridge ESOL Examinations
1 Hills Road
Cambridge CB1 2EU
United Kingdom

Telephone: +44 1223 553355
Fax: +44 1223 460278
e-mail: ESOLHelpdesk@ucles.org.uk

The structure of FCE: an overview

The FCE examination consists of five papers.

Paper 1   Reading   1 hour 15 minutes
This paper consists of **four parts**. Each part contains a text and some questions. Part 4 may contain two or more shorter related texts. There are **35 questions** in total, including multiple choice, gapped text and matching questions.

Paper 2   Writing   1 hour 30 minutes
This paper consists of **two parts** which carry equal marks. For both parts candidates have to write between 120 and 180 words. Part 1 is **compulsory**. It provides texts which are sometimes accompanied by visual material to help in writing a letter.

In Part 2, there are four tasks from which candidates **choose one** to write about. The range of tasks from which questions may be drawn includes an article, a report, a composition, a short story and a letter. The last question is based on the set books. These books remain on the list for two or three years. Look on the website, or contact the Cambridge ESOL Local Secretary in your area for the up-to-date list of set books. The question on the set books has two options from which candidates **choose one** to write about.

Paper 3   Use of English   1 hour 15 minutes
This paper consists of **five parts** and tests control of English grammar, vocabulary and spelling. There are **65 questions** in total. The tasks include gap-filling exercises, sentence transformation, word formation and error correction.

Paper 4   Listening   40 minutes (approximately)
This paper contains **four parts**. Each part contains a recorded text or texts and some questions including multiple choice, sentence completion, true/false and matching. Each text is heard twice. There is a total of **30 questions**.

Paper 5   Speaking   14 minutes
This paper consists of **four parts**. The standard test format is two candidates and two examiners. One examiner takes part in the conversation, the other examiner listens and gives marks. Candidates will be given photographs and other visual material to look at and talk about. Sometimes candidates will talk with the other candidate, sometimes with the examiner and sometimes with both.

Grading

The overall FCE grade is based on the total score gained in all five papers. It is not necessary to achieve a satisfactory level in all five papers in order to pass the examination. Certificates are given to candidates who pass the examination with grade A, B or C. A is the highest. The minimum successful performance in order to achieve a grade C corresponds to about 60% of the total marks. D and E are failing grades. All candidates are sent a Statement of Results which includes a graphical profile of their performance in each paper and shows their relative performance in each one. Each paper is weighted to 40 marks. Therefore, the five FCE papers total 200 marks, after weighting.

For further information on grading and results, go to the website (see page v).

Test 1

PAPER 1   READING (1 hour 15 minutes)

Part 1

You are going to read a magazine article in which a famous chef talks about the importance of good service in restaurants. Choose the most suitable heading from the list **A–I** for each part (**1–7**) of the article. There is one extra heading you do not need to use. There is an example at the beginning (**0**).

Mark your answers **on the separate answer sheet**.

A	A central figure
B	A policy for the times
C	Seen but not heard
D	A fairer system
E	Playing the right part
F	Time well spent
G	A strong sense of involvement
H	The deciding factor
I	All-round improvement

At your service

Top chef and restaurant owner Giancarlo Curtis talks about what he looks for, apart from good food, when he eats out.

0	**I**

Recently, I went into a restaurant near my home where I have eaten several times over the years. It used to have old-fashioned traditional style, but it has just re-opened after being completely renovated. The new surroundings seem to have given a lift to everything, from the food cooked by a new chef from Brittany in France, to the atmosphere and the quality of the service.

1	

Many hours of behind-the-scenes work must have gone into getting the service so good. The staff were very pleasant and the speed with which they reacted to customers' needs was excellent. When someone sneezed, a box of tissues appeared. I have never seen that before in a restaurant. The preparation has certainly paid off.

2	

Twenty years ago when people went out to restaurants, they probably never set eyes on the chef – probably didn't even know his name. But the person they did know was the head waiter. He was the important one, the person who could get you the best table, who could impress your friends by recognising you when you arrived.

3	

Things have changed, but I think what is going to happen with so many good new restaurants opening these days is that the waiters are going to become very important again. The level of service is what is going to distinguish one restaurant from another.

4	**E**

But we are talking about modern, unstuffy service, which is not four waiters hovering around your table making you nervous, but a relaxed presence, giving you the feeling there is someone there and providing help and advice when you need it. There is a fine distinction between a server and a servant, and this is what the best waiter has learnt to appreciate.

5	

Although they have to be commercial, the most popular restaurants aim to provide the kind of reception, comfort and consideration you would give to someone coming for a dinner party at your home. Service is not about the correctness of knives and forks and glasses – people really don't care about those things any more – nowadays it is about putting people at their ease.

6	

What's more, waiting staff need to have a stake in the success of the enterprise. I realised that when I opened my own restaurant. The staff, chefs and waiters did all the decorating and the flowers themselves and it worked well because the right atmosphere had been created by people who cared.

7	

Above all, the waiting staff should be consistent, which is why I have always preferred the custom of putting an optional service charge on the bill, rather than relying on discretionary tips, so that all the staff feel valued. I don't like the kind of situation where there is competition going on, with one star waiter trying to outshine the rest. That affects the quality of the service as a whole.

Part 2

You are going to read a magazine article about an artist who paints flowers. For questions **8–14**, choose the answer (**A**, **B**, **C** or **D**) which you think fits best according to the text.

Mark your answers **on the separate answer sheet**.

An eye for detail

Artist Susan Shepherd is best known for her flower paintings, and the large garden that surrounds her house is the source of many of her subjects. It is full of her favourite flowers, most especially varieties of tulips and poppies. Some of the plants are unruly and seed themselves all over the garden. There is a harmony of colour, shape and structure in the two long flower borders that line the paved path which crosses the garden from east to west.

line 12 Much of this is due to the previous owners, who were keen gardeners, and who left plants that appealed to Susan. She also inherited the gardener, Danny. 'In fact, it was really his garden,' she says. 'We got on very well. At first he would say, "Oh, it's not worth it" to some of the things I wanted to put in, but when I said I wanted to paint them, he recognised what I had in mind.'

Susan prefers to focus on detailed studies of individual plants rather than on the garden as a whole, though she will occasionally paint a group of plants where they are. More usually, she picks them and then takes them up to her studio. 'I don't set the whole thing up at once,' she says. 'I take one flower out and paint it, which might take a few days, and then I bring in another one and build up the painting that way. Sometimes it takes a couple of years to finish.'

Her busiest time of year is spring and early summer, when the tulips are out, followed by the poppies. 'They all come out together, and you're so busy,' she says. But the gradual decaying process is also part of the fascination for her. With tulips, for example, 'you bring them in and put them in water, then leave them for perhaps a day and they each form themselves into different shapes. They open out and are fantastic. When you first put them in a vase, you think they are boring, but they change all the time with twists and turns.'

Susan has always been interested in plants: 'I did botany at school and used to collect wild flowers from all around the countryside,' she says. 'I wasn't particularly interested in gardening then; in fact, I didn't like garden flowers, I thought they were artificial – to me, the only real ones were wild.' Nowadays, the garden owes much to plants that originated in far-off lands, though they seem as much at home in her garden as they did in China or the Himalayas. She has a come-what-may attitude to the garden, rather like an affectionate aunt who is quite happy for children to run about undisciplined as long as they don't do any serious damage.

With two forthcoming exhibitions to prepare for, and a ready supply of subject material at her back door, finding time to work in the garden has been difficult recently. She now employs an extra gardener but, despite the need to paint, she knows that, to maintain her connection with her subject matter, 'you have to get your hands dirty'.

8 In the first paragraph, the writer describes Susan's garden as

    A having caused problems for the previous owners.
    B having a path lined with flowers.
    C needing a lot of work to keep it looking attractive.
    D being only partly finished.

9 What does 'this' in line 12 refer to?

    A the position of the path
    B the number of wild plants
    C the position of the garden
    D the harmony of the planting

10 What does Susan say about Danny?

    A He felt she was interfering in his work.
    B He immediately understood her feelings.
    C He was recommended by the previous owners.
    D He was slow to see the point of some of her ideas.

11 What is Susan's approach to painting?

    A She will wait until a flower is ready to be picked before painting it.
    B She likes to do research on a plant before she paints it.
    C She spends all day painting an individual flower.
    D She creates her paintings in several stages.

12 Susan thinks that tulips

    A are more colourful and better shaped than other flowers.
    B are not easy to paint because they change so quickly.
    C look best some time after they have been cut.
    D should be kept in the house for as long as possible.

13 How does the writer describe Susan's attitude to her garden?

    A She thinks children should be allowed to enjoy it.
    B She prefers planting wild flowers from overseas.
    C She likes a certain amount of disorder.
    D She dislikes criticism of her planting methods.

14 What point is Susan making in the final paragraph?

    A It's essential to find the time to paint even if there is gardening to be done.
    B It's important not to leave the gardening entirely to other people.
    C It's good to have expert help when you grow plants.
    D It's hard to do exhibitions if there are not enough plants ready in the garden.

Part 3

You are going to read a magazine article about swimming with dolphins. Eight paragraphs have been removed from the article. Choose from the paragraphs **A–I** the one which fits each gap (**15–21**). There is one extra paragraph which you do not need to use. There is an example at the beginning (**0**).

Mark your answers **on the separate answer sheet**.

Dolphins in the Bay of Plenty

Swimming with groups of dolphins, known as 'pods', is becoming a popular holiday activity for the adventurous tourist. Our travel correspondent reports.

'You must remember that these dolphins are wild. They are not fed or trained in any way. These trips are purely on the dolphins' terms.' So said one of our guides, as she briefed us before we set out for our rendezvous.

0	I

No skill is required to swim with dolphins, just common sense and an awareness that we are visitors in their world. Once on board the boat, our guides talked to us about what we could expect from our trip.

15	

The common dolphin we were seeking has a blue-black upper body, a grey lower body, and a long snout. We had been told that if they were in a feeding mood we would get a short encounter with them, but if they were being playful then it could last as long as two hours.

16	

Soon we were in the middle of a much larger pod, with dolphins all around us. The first group of six swimmers put on their snorkels, slipped off the back of the boat and swam off towards them.

17	

Visibility was not at its best, but the low clicking sounds and the high-pitched squeaks were amazing enough. The dolphins did not seem bothered by my presence in the water above them. Sometimes they would rush by so close that I could feel the pressure-wave as they passed.

18	

I personally found it more rewarding to sit on the bow of the boat and watch as the surface of the sea all around filled with their perfectly arching dolphin backs. Some of the more advanced snorkellers were able to dive down with these dolphins, an experience they clearly enjoyed.

19	

In fact, they are very sociable animals, always supporting each other within the pod. The guides are beginning to recognise some of the local dolphins by the markings on their backs, and some individuals appear time after time.

20	

Indeed, the pod we had found, on some hidden signal, suddenly turned away from the boat and headed off in the same direction at high speed. We watched as hundreds of backs broke through the water's surface at the same time, disappearing into the distance.

21	

They had finally finished feeding and were content to play alongside as they showed us the way home. The sun beamed down, and as each dolphin broke the surface of the water and exhaled, a rainbow would form for a few seconds in the mist. It was an enchanting experience.

A   This was a magical experience and, as time in the water is limited, everyone rotates to get an equal share. We spent the next two hours getting in and out of the boat, and visiting other pods.

B   An excited shriek led us all to try something that one girl had just discovered, and we all rushed to hang our feet over the front so that the playful creatures would touch them.

C   A spotter plane circled above the bay, looking for large pods of dolphins to direct us towards. On deck, we watched for splashes on the surface of the water.

D   These include mothers gently guiding their young alongside, either to introduce them to the boat, or to proudly show off their babies. Yet, when they become bored with playing, they leave.

E   After 20 minutes, we sighted our first small pod. The dolphins came rushing towards the boat, swimming alongside and overtaking us until they could surf on the boat's bow wave.

F   However, touching the creatures is strongly discouraged. This is despite the fact that dolphins have a very friendly reputation, and have never been known to be aggressive towards human beings in the wild.

G   Eventually it was time to leave, and the boat headed back to port. As we slowly motored along, we picked up another pod, which was joined by more and more dolphins until we had a huge escort.

H   After five minutes, that group was signalled back to the boat. I got ready to slide into the water with the next six swimmers, leaving the excited chatter of the first group behind.

I   I was in Whakatane, in the Bay of Plenty in New Zealand, which is fast becoming the place to visit for those who want a close encounter with dolphins.

Part 4

You are going to read a magazine article in which five people talk about railway journeys. For questions **22–35**, choose from the people (**A–E**). The people may be chosen more than once. When more than one answer is required, these may be given in any order. There is an example at the beginning (**0**).

Mark your answers **on the separate answer sheet**.

Which person or people

found on returning years later that nothing had changed?	**0**	**E**	
was unable to count on the train service?	**22**		
enjoyed the company of fellow passengers?	**23**		
found the views from the train dramatic?	**24**		**25**
welcomed a chance to relax on the trip?	**26**		
was never disappointed by the journey?	**27**		
has a reason for feeling grateful to one special train?	**28**		
travelled on a railway which is no longer in regular service?	**29**		
regretted not going on a particular train trip?	**30**		
used to travel on the railway whenever possible?	**31**		
learnt an interesting piece of information on a train journey?	**32**		
took a train which travelled from one country to another?	**33**		
says that the railway had been looked after by unpaid helpers?	**34**		
was once considered not old enough to travel by train?	**35**		

On the rails

Five celebrities tell Andrew Morgan their favourite memories of railway journeys.

A Andrea Thompson – Newsreader

I fell in love with the south of France a long time ago and try to get back there as often as I can. There's a local train from Cannes along the coast which crosses the border with Italy. It takes you past some of the most amazing seascapes. It never matters what the weather is like, or what time of the year it is, it is always enchanting. Out of the other window are some of the best back gardens and residences in the whole of France. You feel like someone peeping into the property of the rich and famous. The travellers themselves are always lively because there is an interesting mix of tourists and locals, all with different itineraries but all admirers of the breathtaking journey.

B Rod Simpson – Explorer

I have enjoyed so many rail journeys through the years, but if I had to pick a favourite it would be the Nile Valley Express, which runs across the desert of northern Sudan. The one misfortune in my youth, growing up in South Africa, was missing out on a family train journey from Cape Town to the Kruger National Park. I was regarded as being too young and troublesome and was sent off to an aunt. When I came to live in England as a teenager, I still hadn't travelled by train. London Waterloo was the first real station I ever saw and its great glass dome filled me with wonder.

C Betty Cooper – Novelist

I am indebted to one train in particular: the Blue Train, which took my husband and me on our honeymoon across France to catch a boat to Egypt. It was on the train that my husband gave me a pink dress, which I thought was absolutely wonderful. Someone happened to mention that pink was good for the brain, and I've never stopped wearing the colour since. What I remember about the journey itself, however, is how lovely it was to travel through France and then by boat up the Nile to Luxor. It was, without a doubt, the perfect way to wind down after all the wedding preparations.

D Martin Brown – Journalist

We were working on a series of articles based on a round-the-world trip and had to cross a desert in an African country. There wasn't a road, so the only way we could continue our journey was to take what was affectionately known as the Desert Express. The timetable was unreliable – we were just given a day. We also heard that, in any case, the driver would often wait for days to depart if he knew there were passengers still on their way. When it appeared, there was a sudden charge of what seemed like hundreds of people climbing into and onto the carriages – passengers were even allowed to travel on the roof free. During the night, the train crossed some of the most beautiful landscapes I have ever seen. It was like a dream, like travelling across the moon.

E Jennifer Dickens – Actress

I imagine most people's favourite impressions of trains and railways are formed when they are young children, but that's not my case. I was brought up in Singapore and Cyprus, where I saw very few trains, let alone travelled on them. It wasn't until I was a teenager that trains began to dominate my life. I made a film which featured a railway in Yorkshire. Most of the filming took place on an old, disused stretch of the line which had been lovingly maintained by volunteers. That's where my passion for steam trains began. When we weren't filming, we took every opportunity to have a ride on the train, and, when I went back last year, it was as if time had stood still. Everything was the same, even the gas lights on the station platform!

PAPER 2   WRITING (1 hour 30 minutes)

Part 1

You **must** answer this question.

---

1   Your English friend, Bill, is a travel writer and he recently visited a town which you know well. He has written a chapter about the town for a guide book and you have just read the chapter.

Read the extract from Bill's letter and your notes. Then, using all your notes, write a letter to Bill, giving him the information and suggestions he needs.

> *Thanks for agreeing to check the chapter that I've written. Could you let me know what you liked about it? If any of the information is inaccurate, please give me the correct information! Do you think there's anything else I should include?*
>
> *Once again, thanks a lot for reading the chapter. Please write back soon.*
>
> *Bill*

Notes for Bill

Tell Bill what I liked about his chapter – places to visit, …

Give Bill correct information about
– parking in city centre
– museum opening times

Suggest Bill includes
– map
– nightlife (give Bill details)

Write a **letter** of between **120** and **180** words in an appropriate style.
Do not write any postal addresses.

Part 2

Write an answer to **one** of the questions **2–5** in this part. Write your answer in **120–180** words in an appropriate style.

---

2   Your teacher has asked you to write a story for the college English language magazine. The story must **begin** with the following words:

It was only a small mistake but it changed my life for ever.

Write your **story**.

3   You see the following notice in an international magazine.

> # COMPETITION
>
> **Is it better to live in a flat, a modern house or an old house?**
>
> **Write us an article giving your opinions.**
>
> **The best article will be published and the writer will receive £500.**

Write your **article** for the magazine.

4   You have had a class discussion on being rich and famous. Your teacher has now asked you to write a composition, giving your opinions on the following statement:

Everybody would like to be rich and famous.

Write your **composition**.

5   Answer **one** of the following two questions based on your reading of **one** of these set books. Write **(a)** or **(b)** as well as the number **5** in the question box, and the **title** of the book next to the box. Your answer **must** be about one of the books below.

Best Detective Stories of Agatha Christie – Longman Fiction
A Tale of Two Cities – Charles Dickens
Animal Farm – George Orwell
More Tales from Shakespeare – Charles and Mary Lamb
Round the World in Eighty Days – Jules Verne

Either   **(a)**   Which event in the book made the strongest impression on you? Write a **composition** for your teacher describing this event and explaining why it had such an effect on you, with reference to the book or one of the short stories you have read.

Or   **(b)**   'I learnt a lot about how people think and behave from one of the characters in the book.' Do you agree with this statement? Write a **composition**, referring to one of the characters in the book or one of the short stories you have read.

PAPER 3   USE OF ENGLISH (1 hour 15 minutes)

Part 1

For questions **1–15**, read the text below and decide which answer (**A**, **B**, **C** or **D**) best fits each space. There is an example at the beginning (**0**).

Mark your answers **on the separate answer sheet.**

Example:

0   **A** joined   **B** held   **C** were   **D** took

0	A	B	C	D
	—	—	—	▬

THOMAS EDISON

On the night of 21 October 1931, millions of Americans **(0)** ..... part in a coast-to-coast ceremony to commemorate the passing of a great man. Lights **(1)** ..... in homes and offices from New York to California. The ceremony **(2)** ..... the death of an inventor – indeed, to many people, the most important inventor of **(3)** ..... time: Thomas Alva Edison.

Few inventors have **(4)** ..... an impact as great as his on everyday life. While most of his 1,000-plus inventions were devices we no **(5)** ..... use, many of the things he invented played a crucial **(6)** ..... in the development of modern technology, simply by showing what was possible. And one should never **(7)** ..... how amazing some of Edison's inventions were.

In so many ways, Edison is the perfect example of an inventor, by which I **(8)** ..... not just someone who **(9)** ..... up clever gadgets, but someone whose products transform the lives of millions. He possessed the key characteristics that an inventor needs to **(10)** ..... a success of inventions. Sheer determination is certainly one of them. Edison famously tried thousands of materials while working **(11)** ..... a new type of battery, reacting to failure by cheerfully **(12)** ..... to his colleagues: 'Well, **(13)** ..... we know 8,000 things that don't work.' Knowing when to take no **(14)** ..... of experts is also important. Edison's proposal for electric lighting circuitry was **(15)** ..... with total disbelief by eminent scientists, until he lit up whole streets with his lights.

1	**A**	turned out	**B**	came off	**C**	went out	**D**	put off
2	**A**	marked	**B**	distinguished	**C**	noted	**D**	indicated
3	**A**	whole	**B**	full	**C**	entire	**D**	all
4	**A**	put	**B**	had	**C**	served	**D**	set
5	**A**	further	**B**	later	**C**	wider	**D**	longer
6	**A**	effect	**B**	place	**C**	role	**D**	share
7	**A**	underestimate	**B**	lower	**C**	decrease	**D**	mislead
8	**A**	mean	**B**	think	**C**	suppose	**D**	express
9	**A**	creates	**B**	shapes	**C**	dreams	**D**	forms
10	**A**	gain	**B**	make	**C**	achieve	**D**	get
11	**A**	up	**B**	through	**C**	on	**D**	to
12	**A**	announcing	**B**	informing	**C**	instructing	**D**	notifying
13	**A**	by far	**B**	at least	**C**	even though	**D**	for all
14	**A**	notice	**B**	regard	**C**	attention	**D**	view
15	**A**	gathered	**B**	caught	**C**	drawn	**D**	received

Part 2

For questions **16–30**, read the text below and think of the word which best fits each space. Use only **one** word in each space. There is an example at the beginning (**0**).

Write your answers **on the separate answer sheet**.

Example: | 0 | *after* |

VANCOUVER

Vancouver in western Canada is named (**0**) ..*after*.. Captain George Vancouver of the British Royal Navy. However, Captain Vancouver was not the first European (**16**) .... visit the area. The coast (**17**) .... already been explored by the Spanish. Captain Vancouver did (**18**) .... spend many days there, even (**19**) .... he was warmly welcomed by the local people and the scenery amazed him and everyone else (**20**) .... was travelling with him.

The scenery still amazes visitors to (**21**) .... city of Vancouver today. First-time visitors who are (**22**) .... search of breathtaking views (**23**) .... usually directed to a beach which is about ten minutes (**24**) .... the city centre. There, looking out over the sailing boats racing across the blue water, visitors see Vancouver's towering skyline backed by the magnificent Coast Mountains. Then they sigh and say, 'It's (**25**) .... beautiful that I want to stay forever!'

You can't blame them. The city is regularly picked by international travel associations (**26**) .... one of the world's best tourist destinations. They are only confirming what the two million residents and eight million tourists visiting Greater Vancouver (**27**) .... single year already know: there is simply (**28**) .... other place on earth quite (**29**) .... it. It's not just the gorgeous setting where mountains meet the sea that appeals to people, (**30**) .... also Vancouver's wide range of sporting, cultural and entertainment facilities.

Part 3

For questions **31–40**, complete the second sentence so that it has a similar meaning to the first sentence, using the word given. **Do not change the word given**. You must use between **two** and **five** words, including the word given.

Here is an example (**0**).

Example:

0 A very friendly taxi driver drove us into town.

  driven

  We .... a very friendly taxi driver.

The space can be filled by the words 'were driven into town by' so you write:

0	*were driven into town by*

Write **only** the missing words **on the separate answer sheet**.

---

31 'Don't sit in front of the computer for too long,' our teacher told us.

  warned

  Our teacher .... in front of the computer for too long.

32 We got lost coming home from the leisure centre.

  way

  We couldn't .... from the leisure centre.

33 I tried as hard as I could to keep my promise to them.

  best

  I .... break my promise to them.

34 Mary didn't find it difficult to pass her driving test.

  difficulty

  Mary had .... her driving test.

35 I always trust Carla's advice.

somebody

Carla .... advice I always trust.

36 We appear to have been given the wrong address.

as

It .... we have been given the wrong address.

37 I couldn't understand the instructions for my new video recorder.

sense

The instructions for my new video recorder didn't ....
me.

38 Stephen didn't realise that the city centre was a bus ride away.

necessary

What Stephen failed to realise .... to catch a bus to the
city centre.

39 It's a pity we didn't do more sport when I was at school.

could

I wish that .... more sport when I was at school.

40 He described the hotel to us in detail.

detailed

He .... of the hotel.

Part 4

For questions **41–55**, read the text below and look carefully at each line. Some of the lines are correct, and some have a word which should not be there.

If a line is correct, put a tick (✓) by the number **on the separate answer sheet**. If a line has a word which should **not** be there, write the word **on the separate answer sheet**. There are two examples at the beginning (**0** and **00**).

0	✓

Examples:

00	*like*

FRIENDSHIP

0	I believe that nothing matters as much as having a couple of really good
00	friends. They help you feel like good about yourself and they'll always
41	listen to your problems for hours on end. Since there are friends for different
42	reasons, for different ages and stages in life. New made friends and 'best'
43	friends, friends for playing tennis and going to the cinema with – all
44	of us are dependent on having friends. So how and why do we make up
45	friends? Psychologists tell us that we prefer those we see as sharing with
46	our views and attitudes and who are similar to us in an age and background,
47	though not necessarily in any personality. We see our friends as reflecting
48	ourselves, or that what we would like to be. This can be particularly
49	important when we are teenagers. Many of people – and I'm no exception –
50	regard their oldest friends as their closest. I have a friend so that
51	I've known since some schooldays. She lives in Australia and we
52	rarely see much each other. However, on my last birthday we got together
53	in Paris and have spent a wonderful weekend sightseeing and talking.
54	We will know that, no matter how many years go by when we do not
55	get together at all, the same level of friendship always remains.

Part 5

For questions **56–65**, read the text below. Use the word given in capitals at the end of each line to form a word that fits in the space in the **same** line. There is an example at the beginning (**0**).

Write your answers **on the separate answer sheet**.

Example:	0	*amazement*

A JOB WITH RISKS

Have you ever been to the cinema and wondered in (**0**) *amazement* how	**AMAZE**
film stars manage to perform (**56**) .... acts like jumping off buildings or driving	**DANGER**
at great speed? They don't, of course. The real (**57**) .... are usually stunt men	**PERFORM**
or women, who can earn a very good (**58**) .... by standing in	**LIVE**
for the stars when necessary. The work is (**59**) .... demanding and, before	**INCREDIBLE**
qualifying for this job, they have to (**60**) .... their ability in six sports including	**PROOF**
skiing, riding and gymnastics.	
Naturally, (**61**) .... and timing are important and everything is planned down	**SAFE**
to the (**62**) .... detail. In a scene which involves a complicated series of	**TINY**
actions, there is no time for (**63**) .... mistakes. A stunt man or woman often	**CARE**
has only one chance of getting things right, (**64**) .... film stars, who can	**LIKE**
always film a scene (**65**) .... until it gains the director's approval.	**REPEAT**

PAPER 4   LISTENING (approximately 40 minutes)

Part 1

You will hear people talking in eight different situations. For questions **1–8**, choose the best answer (**A**, **B** or **C**).

---

1   You overhear a young man talking about his first job.
How did he feel in his first job?

   A   bored

   B   confused

   C   enthusiastic

          1

2   You hear a radio announcement about a dance company.
What are listeners being invited to?

   A   a show

   B   a talk

   C   a party

          2

3   You overhear a woman talking to a man about something that happened to her.
Who was she?

   A   a pedestrian

   B   a driver

   C   a passenger

          3

4   You hear a woman talking on the radio about her work making wildlife films.
What is her main point?

   A   Being in the right place at the right time is a matter of luck.

   B   More time is spent planning than actually filming.

   C   It is worthwhile spending time preparing.

          4

5   You hear part of a travel programme on the radio.
    Where is the speaker?

    A   outside a café

    B   by the sea

    C   on a lake

6   You overhear a woman talking about a table-tennis table in a sports shop.
    What does she want the shop assistant to do about her table-tennis table?

    A   provide her with a new one

    B   have it put together for her

    C   give her the money back

7   You hear part of an interview with a businesswoman.
    What is her business?

    A   hiring out boats

    B   hiring out caravans

    C   building boats

8   You hear a man talking on the radio.
    Who is talking?

    A   an actor

    B   a journalist

    C   a theatre-goer

Part 2

You will hear a radio interview with Mike Reynolds, whose hobby is exploring underground places such as caves. For questions **9–18**, complete the sentences.

Cavers explore underground places such as mines and

	9

as well as caves.

When cavers camp underground, they choose places which have

	and	**10**

available.

In the UK, the place Mike likes best for caving is

	11

As a physical activity, Mike compares caving to

	12

Cavers can pay as much as £20 for a suitable

	13

Cavers can pay as much as £50 for the right kind of

	14

, which is worn on the head.

Mike recommends buying expensive

	15

to avoid having accidents.

Caving is a sport for people of

	16

and backgrounds.

Some caves in Britain are called 'places of

	' **17**

The need for safety explains why people don't organise caving

	18

Part 3

You will hear five different people talking about their work on a cruise ship. For questions **19–23**, choose from the list (**A–F**) what each speaker says about their work. Use the letters only once. There is one extra letter which you do not need to use.

A One aspect of my job is less interesting than others.

Speaker 1 | 19 |

B My job involves planning for the unexpected.

Speaker 2 | 20 |

C You have to be sociable to do my job.

Speaker 3 | 21 |

D I don't like routine in my working life.

Speaker 4 | 22 |

E There's not much work to do during the day.

Speaker 5 | 23 |

F I provide passengers with a souvenir of their trip.

Part 4

You will hear a radio discussion in which four people are talking about the advertising of children's toys on television. For questions **24–30**, decide which views are expressed by any of the speakers and which are not. Write **YES** for those views which are expressed, and **NO** for those which are not expressed.

---

24 Most young children are aware when advertisements are being shown on television.

	24

25 There are fewer toy advertisements on British television than there used to be.

	25

26 Parents are spending increasing amounts of their money on traditional toys.

	26

27 Advertisers have to indicate the actual size of toys advertised on television.

	27

28 Children would be less influenced by toy advertisements if they were only shown after 8.00 pm.

	28

29 Advertising encourages children to lose interest in their toys very quickly.

	29

30 Evidence shows that most people are worried about toy advertising on television.

	30

PAPER 5   SPEAKING (14 minutes)

You take the Speaking test with another candidate, referred to here as your partner. There are two examiners. One will speak to you and your partner and the other will be listening. Both examiners will award marks.

Part 1 (3 minutes)

The examiner asks you and your partner questions about yourselves. You may be asked about things like 'your home town', 'your interests', 'your career plans', etc.

Part 2 (4 minutes)

The examiner gives you two photographs and asks you to talk about them for one minute. The examiner then asks your partner a question about your photographs and your partner responds briefly.

Then the examiner gives your partner two different photographs. Your partner talks about these photographs for one minute. This time the examiner asks you a question about your partner's photographs and you respond briefly.

Part 3 (approximately 3 minutes)

The examiner asks you and your partner to talk together. You may be asked to solve a problem or try to come to a decision about something. For example, you might be asked to decide the best way to use some rooms in a language school. The examiner gives you a picture to help you but does not join in the conversation.

Part 4 (approximately 4 minutes)

The examiner joins in the conversation. You all talk together in a more general way about what has been said in Part 3. The examiner asks you questions but you and your partner are also expected to develop the conversation.

Test 2

PAPER 1   READING (1 hour 15 minutes)

M: 40

Part 1

You are going to read a newspaper article about an island in the Irish Sea, called the Isle of Man, which is fast becoming a centre for film-making. Choose from the list **A–H** the sentence which best summarises each part (**1–6**) of the article. There is one extra sentence which you do not need to use. There is an example at the beginning (**0**).

Mark your answers **on the separate answer sheet**.

A	The new film industry is not expected to make big profits immediately.
B	The new film industry has resulted in some criticism of the island's government.
C	It was initially difficult to persuade film-makers to use the island.
D	The island is already able to compete with other film-making centres.
E	Film-makers are able to find a wide range of settings for their films on the island.
F	More investment is planned as the new film industry becomes established.
G	Financial reasons have made film companies see the island as a good place to make new films.
H	The island's inhabitants are keen to be involved with the new film industry.

TREASURE ISLAND

0	H

Only 73,000 people live on the Isle of Man, but several thousand of them have registered with Jay-Dee Promotions. This is the casting and extras agency John Banks and his wife Pat run to service the film industry that has suddenly taken off on the island. Banks does not know exactly how many clients he has – he is too busy to count them. And Jay-Dee is only one of three such agencies that have sprung up in the last year or two.

1	G

Until recently the island's principal contributions to cinema were a comedy about motorcycle racing, and *The Manxman*, one of Alfred Hitchcock's silent movies. But producers have now discovered an important reason to undertake the inconvenient voyage to the middle of the Irish Sea – money. In the past couple of years, the Isle of Man government has lent over £6.5 million of public money to film companies. If a film is a success then the Isle of Man will receive a share of the profits. This has turned the island into an offshore Hollywood.

2	A

Only one film was made in 1995, two in 1996, but there were no fewer than eleven in the following year. However, from the beginning, the Isle of Man government has followed the strategy of Hollywood, where the rule of thumb is that for every ten films, seven will lose money, one will cover its costs, one will provide modest returns, and the tenth, it is hoped, will be an enormous hit.

3	E D

An island 45 kilometres long, with no history of film production, is suddenly turning out the same number of films as the Scottish film industry, which has a huge pool of local talent and an infrastructure that has evolved over the years. However, it was always the intention of the Isle of Man government to lure productions away from England, Scotland and Ireland.

4	E

Producers have suddenly discovered the affluent little holiday island to be the perfect location for seemingly any film. It has doubled for Cornwall, Hamburg, Sydney Harbour in the nineteenth century, rural Ireland and inner-city England. It has even attracted a new production of *Treasure Island*. Geographical specifics did not seem to be uppermost in the mind of the film's producer: 'We gambled with the fact that we would be able to have enough sunny days to be able to do the tropical island part.'

5	C ?

The Isle of Man film initiative was inspired not by vague dreams of glory, but by hopes of boosting the economy. Its tourist industry has been in decline for twenty years and it was thought that a hit film would help it. One of the early objectives was simply to demonstrate to a doubtful film industry that it was possible to make feature films on the island.

6	F

The government's financial advisors have targeted films in the £2–3 million price range as promising the highest potential returns at least risk. The Isle of Man is an important financial centre and this expertise has aided its move into film. The island's government has another £6.5 million to lend over the next two years and is currently considering building a studio.

Part 2

You are going to read an extract from a novel. For questions **7–13**, choose the answer (**A**, **B**, **C** or **D**) which you think fits best according to the text.

Mark your answers **on the separate answer sheet**.

Miss Rita Cohen, a tiny, pale-skinned girl who looked half the age of Seymour's daughter, Marie, but claimed to be some six years older, came to his factory one day. She was dressed in overalls and ugly big shoes, and a bush of wiry hair framed her pretty face. She was so tiny, so young that he could barely believe that she was at the University of Pennsylvania, doing research into the leather industry in New Jersey for her Master's degree.

Three or four times a year someone either phoned Seymour or wrote to him to ask permission to see his factory, and occasionally he would assist a student by answering questions over the phone or, if the student struck him as especially serious, by offering a brief tour.

Rita Cohen was nearly as small, he thought, as the children from Marie's third-year class, who'd been brought the 50 kilometres from their rural schoolhouse one day, all those years ago, so that Marie's daddy could show them how he made gloves, show them especially Marie's favourite spot, the laying-off table, where, at the end of the process, the men shaped and pressed each and every glove by pulling it carefully down over steam-heated brass hands. The hands were dangerously hot

line 14 and they were shiny and they stuck straight up from the table in a row, thin-looking, like hands that had been flattened. As a little girl, Marie was captivated by their strangeness and called them the 'pancake hands'.

He heard Rita asking, 'How many pieces come in a shipment?' 'How many? Between twenty and twenty-five thousand.' She continued taking notes as she asked, 'They come direct to your shipping department?'

He liked finding that she was interested in every last detail. 'They come to the tannery. The tannery is a contractor. We buy the material and they make it into the right kind of leather for us to use. My grandfather and father worked in the tannery right here in town. So did I, for six months, when I started in the business. Ever been inside a tannery?' 'Not yet.' 'Well, you've got to go to a tannery if you're going to write about leather. I'll set that up for you if you'd like that. They're primitive places. The technology has improved things, but what you'll see isn't that different from what you'd have seen hundreds of years ago. Awful work. It's said to be the oldest industry of which remains have been found anywhere. Six-thousand-year-old relics of tanning found somewhere – Turkey, I believe. The first clothing was just skins that were tanned by smoking them. I told you it was an interesting subject once you get into it. My father is the leather scholar; he's the one you should be talking to. Start my father off about gloves and he'll talk for two days. That's typical, by the way: glovemen love the trade and everything about it. Tell me, have you ever seen anything being manufactured, Miss Cohen?' 'I can't say I have.' 'Never seen anything made?' 'Saw my mother make a cake when I was a child.'

He laughed. She had made him laugh. An innocent with spirit, eager to learn. His daughter was easily 30 cm taller than Rita Cohen, fair where she was dark, but otherwise Rita Cohen had begun to remind him of Marie. The good-natured intelligence that would just waft out of her and into the house when she came home from school, full of what she'd learned in class. How she remembered everything. Everything neatly taken down in her notebook and memorised overnight.

'I'll tell you what we're going to do. We're going to bring you right through the whole process. Come on. We're going to make you a pair of gloves and you're going to watch them being made from start to finish. What size do you wear?'

7   What was Seymour's first impression of Rita Cohen?

   A   She reminded him of his daughter.
   B   She was rather unattractive.
   C   She did not look like a research student.
   D   She hadn't given much thought to her appearance.

8   Seymour would show students round his factory if

   A   he thought they were genuinely interested.
   B   they telephoned for permission.
   C   they wrote him an interesting letter.
   D   their questions were hard to answer by phone.

9   What did Seymour's daughter like most about visiting the factory?

   A   watching her father make gloves
   B   helping to shape the gloves
   C   making gloves for her schoolfriends
   D   seeing the brass hands

10   The word 'shiny' in line 14 describes

   A   the look of the hands.
   B   the size of the hands.
   C   the feel of the hands.
   D   the temperature of the hands.

11   Seymour says that most tanneries today

   A   have been running for over a hundred years.
   B   are located in very old buildings.
   C   are dependent on older workers.
   D   still use traditional methods.

12   What does Seymour admire about his father?

   A   his educational background
   B   his knowledge of history
   C   his enthusiasm for the business
   D   his skill as a glovemaker

13   When she was a schoolgirl, Marie

   A   made her parents laugh.
   B   was intelligent but lazy.
   C   easily forgot what she had learned.
   D   was hard-working and enthusiastic.

Part 3

You are going to read a newspaper article about human beings getting taller. Eight sentences have been removed from the article. Choose from the sentences **A–I** the one that fits each gap (**14–20**). There is one extra sentence which you do not need to use. There is an example at the beginning (**0**).

Mark your answers **on the separate answer sheet**.

It's true – we're all getting too big for our boots

Chris Greener was fourteen when he told his careers teacher he wanted to join the navy when he left school. 'What do you want to be?' asked the teacher, looking the boy up and down. 'The flagpole on a ship?' The teacher had a point – because Chris, though still only fourteen, was already almost two metres tall. **0** **I**

Every decade, the average height of people in Europe grows another centimetre. Every year, more and more truly big people are born. Intriguingly, this does not mean humanity is producing a new super race. **14** Only now are we losing the effects of generations of poor diet – with dramatic effects. 'We are only now beginning to fulfil our proper potential and are reaching the dimensions programmed by our bodies,' says palaeontologist Professor Chris Stringer. 'We are becoming Cro-Magnons again – the people who lived on this planet 40,000 years ago.'

For most of human history, our ancestors got their food from a wide variety of sources: women gathered herbs, fruits and berries, while men supplemented these with occasional kills of animals (a way of life still adopted by the world's few remaining tribes of hunter-gatherers). **15** Then about 9,000 years ago, agriculture was invented – with devastating consequences. Most of the planet's green places have been gradually taken over by farmers, with the result that just three carbohydrate-rich plants – wheat, rice and maize – provide more than half of the calories consumed by the human race today.

16 Over the centuries we have lived on soups, porridges and breads that have left us underfed and underdeveloped. In one study of skeletons of American Indians in Ohio, scientists discovered that when they began to grow corn, healthy hunter-gatherers were turned into sickly, underweight farmers. Tooth decay increased, as did diseases. Far from being one of the blessings of the New World, corn was a public health disaster, according to some anthropologists.

17 The fact that most people relying on this system are poorly nourished and stunted has only recently been tackled, even by the world's wealthier nations. Only in Europe, the US and Japan are diets again reflecting the richness of our ancestors' diets.

As a result, the average man in the US is now 179cm, in Holland 180cm, and in Japan 177cm. It is a welcome trend, though not without its own problems. **18** A standard bed-length has remained at 190cm since 1860, while the height of a door was fixed at 198cm in 1880. Even worse, leg-room in planes and trains seems to have shrunk rather than grown, while clothes manufacturers are constantly having to revise their range of products.

The question is: where will it all end? We cannot grow for ever. **19** But what is it? According to Robert Fogel, of Chicago University, it could be as much as 193cm – and we are likely to reach it some time this century.

However, scientists add one note of qualification. Individuals may be growing taller because of improved nutrition, but as a species we are actually shrinking, although very slightly. During the last ice age, 10,000 years ago, members of the human race were slightly rounder and taller – an evolutionary response to the cold. (Large round bodies are best at keeping in heat.) **20** And as the planet continues to heat up, we may shrink even further. In other words, the growth of human beings could be offset by global warming.

A   We must have some programmed upper limit.

B   As they benefit from the changes in agriculture, people expect to have this wide variety of foods available.

C   In fact, we are returning to what we were like as cavemen.

D   This poor diet has had a disastrous effect on human health and physique.

E   Since the climate warmed, we appear to have got slightly thinner and smaller, even when properly fed.

F   Nevertheless, from then on agriculture spread because a piece of farmed land could support ten times the number of people who had previously lived off it as hunter-gatherers.

G   One research study found that they based their diet on 85 different wild plants, for example.

H   Heights may have risen, but the world has not moved on, it seems.

I   Today, at 228cm, he is Britain's tallest man.

Activate Learning

Part 4

You are going to read an article about guidebooks to London. For questions **21–35**, choose from the guidebooks (**A–G**). The guidebooks may be chosen more than once. When more than one answer is required, these may be given in any order. There is an example at the beginning (**0**).

Mark your answers **on the separate answer sheet**.

Of which guidebook(s) is the following stated?

It is frequently revised. | **0** | **F**

It is quite expensive. | **21** | B

It is not aimed at local people. | **22** | F

Its appearance is similar to other books by the same publisher. | **23**

It contains some errors. | **24**

It is reasonably priced. | **25** | E

It shows great enthusiasm for the city. | **26** | N

It has always been produced with a particular market in mind. | **27** | F

It is written by people who have all the latest information. | A | **28**

It is written in a friendly style. | A | **29** | **30** | G

It is part of the first series of its kind to be published. | B | **31**

It omits some sights which should be included. | **32** | F

It contains more information than other guides. | **33**

It might appeal to London residents. | **34**

Its information about places to eat is enjoyable to read. | **35**

London Guidebooks

Visitors to London, which has so much to offer, need all the help they can get. Alastair Bickley takes his pick of the capital's guidebooks.

Guidebook A

Informal and familiar in tone, this valuable book has much to offer. Produced by the same people who put together London's principal listings magazine, this is right up to date with what's happening in the city – very much its home ground. It is concise enough to cater for those staying for just a couple of days, yet covers all areas of interest to visitors in an admirably condensed and approachable way. On balance, this is the single most handy book to have with you in London.

Guidebook B

This book is beautifully illustrated, with cutaway diagrams of buildings and bird's-eye-view itineraries rather than plain maps. This is a model of the clear professional design that is the recognisable trademark of this series. Its coverage of the main sights is strong, and visually it's a real treat – a delight to own as a practical guide. It's a bit pricey but well worth a look.

Guidebook C

Probably the best-suited for a longish stay in the city. This guide surpasses its competitors in its sheer depth of knowledge and in the detail it provides. It's particularly handy for the thorough stroller with plenty of time on his or her hands, covering virtually every building or monument of any interest – and with well-drawn maps of each area. Its coverage of all types of restaurants, which encourages you to go out and try them, can also be appreciated from the comfort of your armchair.

Guidebook D

In many ways, this serviceable guide is broadly comparable to the other guides but, whereas many of them feel as though they come from the 'inside', this feels geared towards visitors from elsewhere in the English-speaking world. It has its strengths, offering decent coverage of the sights, museums and inexpensive places to eat.

Guidebook E

It is astonishing – and perhaps the greatest tribute one can pay to London as a city – that it's possible to have a high-quality holiday there and scarcely spend anything on admission charges. In this guide, the obvious bargains (National Gallery, British Museum, etc.) are almost lost among an impressive range of places which cost nothing to visit. It should pay more attention to the numerous wonderful churches in the City of London but otherwise this is a must for the seriously budget-conscious or the Londoner who is looking for something different (like me). The book itself isn't quite free, but at £4.95, it's not far off it.

Guidebook F

This is the latest in the longest-standing series of budget guides and, unlike its competitors, it is still definitely aimed at young backpackers. Its description of the sights is less detailed than most and the accuracy of some of the information is surprisingly poor for such a regularly updated publication. However, it manages to cram in everything of significance, and is strongly weighted towards practicalities and entertainment.

Guidebook G

Here is a guide which comes with a distinct personality rather than following the style of the series to which it belongs. It is chatty, companionable, opinionated, crammed full of history and anecdotes as well as practical information. I can best describe the experience (for that's what it is) of reading this book as follows: imagine arriving in town and being taken in hand by a local who is determined to show you the best of everything and to give you the benefit of their considerable experience of a city for which they obviously hold a passion.

PAPER 2   WRITING (1 hour 30 minutes)

Part 1

You **must** answer this question.

---

1   Some British people are coming to your area and you have been asked to help organise the group's visit.

Read the extract from a letter you have received from Mrs Davidson, the leader of the group, and the notes you have made. Then write a letter to Mrs Davidson, using all your notes.

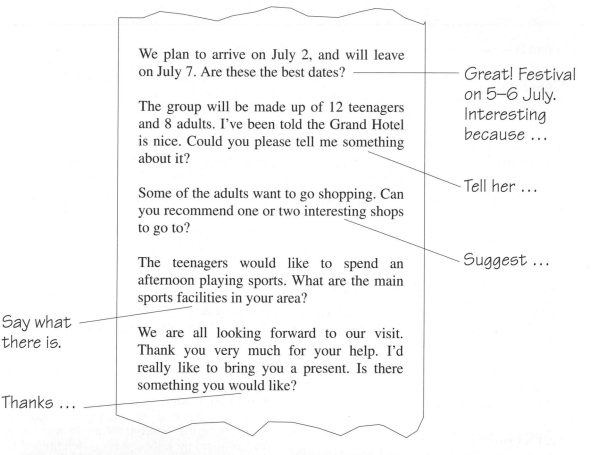

We plan to arrive on July 2, and will leave on July 7. Are these the best dates? —— Great! Festival on 5–6 July. Interesting because ...

The group will be made up of 12 teenagers and 8 adults. I've been told the Grand Hotel is nice. Could you please tell me something about it? —— Tell her ...

Some of the adults want to go shopping. Can you recommend one or two interesting shops to go to? —— Suggest ...

The teenagers would like to spend an afternoon playing sports. What are the main sports facilities in your area? —— Say what there is.

We are all looking forward to our visit. Thank you very much for your help. I'd really like to bring you a present. Is there something you would like? —— Thanks ...

Write a **letter** of between **120** and **180** words in an appropriate style.
Do not write any postal addresses.

Part 2

Write an answer to **one** of the questions **2–5** in this part. Write your answer in **120–180** words in an appropriate style.

---

2   You have seen this announcement in an international music magazine.

> ### MUSIC ON THE RADIO
>
> Our readers tell us they love listening to music on the radio! What would your ideal evening music programme consist of? Write us an article:
> - telling us what type of music you'd like to hear
> - giving your suggestions for making the programme popular
>
> The writer with the best ideas will win £1,000 to spend on CDs.

Write your **article**.

3   You have had a class discussion on how people's lives will change in the future. Now your teacher has asked you to write a composition on the following statement:

People's lives will change dramatically in the next 50 years.

Write your **composition**.

4   An English friend, Jo, has written to you for some advice. This is part of the letter you have received.

> *I leave school this summer and have a year free before university. I want to come to your country. First I'd like to spend some time travelling. Then I'd like to find a job for three months. Please give me some advice on travelling and working in your country.*
>
> *Thanks, Jo*

Write your **letter**. Do not write any postal addresses.

5   Answer **one** of the following two questions based on your reading of **one** of these set books. Write **(a)** or **(b)** as well as the number **5** in the question box, and the **title** of the book next to the box. Your answer **must** be about one of the books below.

Best Detective Stories of Agatha Christie – Longman Fiction
A Tale of Two Cities – Charles Dickens
Animal Farm – George Orwell
More Tales from Shakespeare – Charles and Mary Lamb
Round the World in Eighty Days – Jules Verne

Either   (a)   'In a story, the places are often more important than the people.' How true is this of the book or one of the short stories you have read? Write a **composition** giving your opinions.

Or   (b)   You have agreed to write an **article** for your college magazine on the book you have read. Write about an important day for one of the characters in the book or one of the short stories you have read. You should also explain why this day was important for the character.

PAPER 3   USE OF ENGLISH (1 hour 15 minutes)

Part 1

For questions **1–15**, read the text below and decide which answer (**A, B, C** or **D**) best fits each space. There is an example at the beginning (**0**).

Mark your answers **on the separate answer sheet**.

Example:

0   A face   **B** outline   **C** surface   **D** top

0	A	B	C	D
	▄▄	▭	▭	▭

UNDER THE CITY STREETS

While skyscraper offices and elegant apartment blocks remain the public **(0)** ..... of most major cities, these cities also have a mass of secret tunnels and hidden pipes below **(1)** ..... which keep everything working. This other world exists beneath many of our greatest cities, forgotten or neglected by all but a tiny **(2)** ..... of engineers and historians.

For example, there are more than 150 kilometres of rivers under the streets of London. Most have been **(3)** ..... over and, sadly, all that **(4)** ..... is their names. Perhaps the greatest **(5)** ..... to the city is the River Fleet, a **(6)** ..... great river which previously had beautiful houses on its **(7)** ..... . It now goes underground in the north of the city and **(8)** ..... into the River Thames by Blackfriars Bridge.

The London Underground **(9)** ..... 1000 kilometres of underground railway track winding under the capital and more than 100 stations below street level. Along some underground railway **(10)** ..... , commuters can sometimes catch a **(11)** ..... glimpse of the platforms of more than forty closed stations which have been left under the city. **(12)** ..... some are used as film sets, most **(13)** ..... forgotten. Some have had their entrances on the street turned into restaurants and shops, but most entrances have been **(14)** ..... down. Interestingly, there is also a special underground Post Office railway that **(15)** ..... a link between east and west London postal centres.

1 **A** land   **B** ground   **C** soil   **D** earth

2 **A** number   **B** amount   **C** total   **D** few

3 **A** covered   **B** protected   **C** hidden   **D** sheltered

4 **A** stays   **B** stops   **C** remains   **D** keeps

5 **A** miss   **B** absence   **C** waste   **D** loss

6 **A** once   **B** past   **C** then   **D** prior

7 **A** borders   **B** coasts   **C** banks   **D** rims

8 **A** gets   **B** flows   **C** leaks   **D** lets

9 **A** holds   **B** contains   **C** has   **D** consists

10 **A** lanes   **B** avenues   **C** paths   **D** lines

11 **A** rapid   **B** brief   **C** fast   **D** sharp

12 **A** Despite   **B** Unless   **C** Although   **D** Since

13 **A** lie   **B** last   **C** live   **D** lay

14 **A** pulled   **B** broken   **C** brought   **D** cut

15 **A** occurs   **B** provides   **C** gives   **D** results

Part 2

For questions **16–30**, read the text below and think of the word which best fits each space. Use only **one** word in each space. There is an example at the beginning (**0**).

Write your answers **on the separate answer sheet**.

Example:

0	*the*

MY HOME TOWN

I was born in one of (**0**) ....*the*.... most interesting cities in Malaysia. It has a rich, colourful history and many parts of the city have hardly changed at (**16**) .... during the last five centuries. However, nowadays, it is (**17**) .... longer the trade centre that it once (**18**) .... It is difficult to imagine that at one time its harbour (**19**) .... to be visited by over 2,000 ships a week, and that the huge warehouses along the quayside would have (**20**) .... full of spices and silks, jewels and tea.

The old city centre is small, which (**21**) .... it very easy to explore (**22**) .... foot. A river neatly divides the town, (**23**) .... only physically but in spirit too. On one side, you find a (**24**) .... many grand houses, but immediately you cross the river, you find (**25**) .... in ancient Chinatown, which is where you really (**26**) .... a step back into the past.

From the earliest times, this has been the heart of the city and it's fun to wander through the colourful, noisy backstreets. As (**27**) .... as the streets that sell a wide (**28**) .... of clothes and shoes, there are also streets famous (**29**) .... high quality antiques. Unfortunately, most of the bargains disappeared many years ago. However, (**30**) .... you look around carefully, you could still come across an interesting souvenir.

Part 3

For questions **31–40**, complete the second sentence so that it has a similar meaning to the first sentence, using the word given. **Do not change the word given**. You must use between **two** and **five** words, including the word given.

Here is an example (**0**).

Example:

0   A very friendly taxi driver drove us into town.

driven

We .... a very friendly taxi driver.

The space can be filled by the words 'were driven into town by' so you write:

0	*were driven into town by*

Write **only** the missing words on **the separate answer sheet**.

---

31   Nina's parents said she wasn't to use their new camera.

let

Nina's parents .... use their new camera.

32   The TV programme was so complicated that none of the children could understand it.

too

The TV programme was .... the children to understand.

33   The only shoes I could find to fit me were in black leather.

any

I could .... fitted me, apart from some in black leather.

34   Luke knocked over the old lady's bicycle by accident.

mean

Luke .... knock over the old lady's bicycle.

35 I've already planned my next holiday.

arrangements

I've already ~~made the arrangements for~~ my next holiday.

36 They say the ice in Antarctica is getting thinner all the time.

said

The ice in Antarctica ~~is said that is~~ getting thinner all the time.

37 We didn't enjoy our walk along the seafront because it was so windy.

prevented

The strong wind ~~prevented us for enjoying~~ our walk along the seafront.

38 It looks as if Susan has left her jacket behind.

seems

Susan ~~seems to have left~~ her jacket behind.

39 A newly-qualified dentist took out Mr Dupont's tooth.

had

Mr Dupont ~~had a tooth~~ by a newly-qualified dentist.

40 Antonio only lost the 100-metre race because he fell.

not

If Antonio had ~~not fallen he would have~~ won the 100-metre race.

Part 4

For questions **41–55**, read the text below and look carefully at each line. Some of the lines are correct, and some have a word which should not be there.

If a line is correct, put a tick (✓) by the number **on the separate answer sheet**. If a line has a word which should **not** be there, write the word **on the separate answer sheet**. There are two examples at the beginning (**0** and **00**).

0	✓

Examples:

00	*nevertheless*

PLAYING CHESS

0	In your last letter you asked me to tell you why I like playing
00	chess so much. Well, I nevertheless think it is because chess gives
41	me a feeling of the excitement. I am quite competitive and like
42	the challenge of playing one-to-one. It gets intense sometimes;
43	in a game you can get extremely nervous and excited and have all
44	sorts of emotions. If I have played such a good player, put up
45	a good fight and lost, then that is too satisfying, but it is always
46	better than to win! There is also a good social side to chess. I
47	have made lots of friends at playing in competitions across
48	Europe. It is really interesting seeing cultures more different from
49	mine and trying to practise other languages! Now I play most of
50	weekends and holidays, but I do not know for certain if I will continue
51	to take part in competitions. During the last couple of years while I
52	have had more schoolwork, in which makes life more difficult. You
53	have got to be an extremely good player for chess to be so financially
54	worthwhile. However, I would like recommend it as a hobby to
55	anyone. If you are interested, you should to join a chess club at once.

Part 5

For questions **56–65**, read the text below. Use the word given in capitals at the end of each line to form a word that fits in the space in the **same** line. There is an example at the beginning (**0**).

Write your answers **on the separate answer sheet**.

Example:	**0**	*existence*

BIGFOOT

There are some people who believe in the (**0**) ....*existence*.... of Bigfoot, **EXIST**

a (**56**) .... ape-like creature that is supposed to live in the mountains **MYSTERY**

of the USA. In 1967, some hunters claimed to have (**57**) .... filmed **ACCIDENT**

such a creature and many people see this as firm (**58**) .... that **PROVE**

Bigfoot is real.

But now, researchers have come to the (**59**) .... that the film is a trick. **CONCLUDE**

After a close (**60**) .... of it, they claim to have identified a man-made **ANALYSE**

fastener at the creature's waist. Bigfoot is, therefore, (**61**) .... to be **LIKELY**

anything more than a man in an animal suit.

Some people remain unconvinced by the (**62**) .... , though. Bigfoot fans **SCIENCE**

are extremely (**63**) .... that a fastener would show up on such an old film. **DOUBT**

In (**64**) .... , they say that the creature caught on camera does not move **ADD**

like a human and that it is therefore (**65**) .... a wild creature of nature. **TRUE**

The debate goes on.

Visual materials for Paper 5

1A

1B

1E

1C

1D

2A

2B

2E

2C

2D

3A

3B

3E

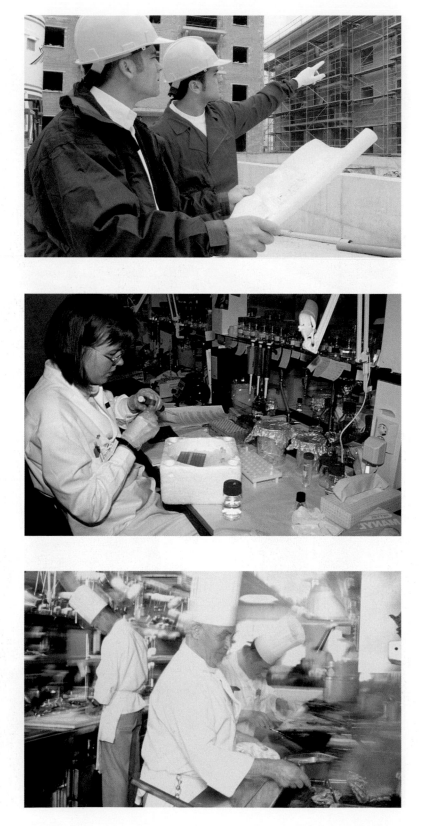

3C

3D

4A

4B

4E

4C

4D

PAPER 4   LISTENING (approximately 40 minutes)

Part 1

You will hear people talking in eight different situations. For questions **1–8**, choose the best answer (**A**, **B** or **C**).

1   You hear part of an interview in which a film director talks about his favourite movie.
     Why does he like the film?

    A   It is very funny.

    B   It is very exciting.

    C   It is very romantic.

	1

2   You hear a man talking about a sofa he bought.
     What is he complaining about?

    A   He received the wrong sofa.

    B   The shop overcharged him for the sofa.

    C   The sofa was damaged.

	2

3   You hear an actor talking about using different accents in his work.
     What point is he making about actors?

    A   They need to study a wide variety of accents.

    B   They have to be able to control their use of accents.

    C   They should try to keep their original accents.

	3

4   You hear part of an interview in which a man is talking about winning his first horse race.
     What does he say about it?

    A   He found it rather disappointing.

    B   He didn't have a chance to celebrate.

    C   He was too tired to care.

	4

5 You hear a writer of musicals talking on the radio.
What is he trying to explain?

    A   why his aunt's career was not very successful

    B   the difference between American and British musicals

    C   his reasons for becoming a writer of musicals

6 You hear the beginning of a lecture about ancient history.
What is the lecture going to be about?

    A   trade in arms and weapons

    B   trade in luxury household goods

    C   trade in works of art

7 You hear a man talking about travelling from London to France for his job.
What does he say about the train journey?

    A   He's able to use it to his advantage.

    B   It's a boring but necessary part of his job.

    C   He enjoys the social aspect of it.

8 You hear a woman in a shop talking about some lost photographs.
What does she think the shop should give her?

    A   some money

    B   a replacement film

    C   an apology

Part 2

You will hear part of a radio interview with a woman who sailed round the world on her own. For questions **9–18**, complete the sentences.

Anna was employed by a [_____ **9**] when she first started sailing.

The idea of sailing round the world came from a book called

[_____ **10**]

Anna spent some time [_____ **11**] the boat before taking it out to sea.

Anna tested her boat on a trip which lasted for only

[_____ **12**] because it was damaged.

Anna got the money she needed to make the trip from various

[_____ **13**] companies.

Anna's worst problem during the trip was when she felt

[_____ **14**] because the boat was going so slowly.

Anna found the

[_____ **15**] in the Southern Ocean the most exciting part of the trip.

On her return, Anna phoned the [_____ **16**] to ask for a certificate.

Anna's claim was doubted because she hadn't been in contact with people on

[_____ **17**] during her trip.

Anna's story was finally believed after her

[_____ **18**] had been checked.

Part 3

You will hear five young people talking about what makes a good teacher. For questions **19–23**, choose from the list (**A–F**) which of the opinions each speaker expresses. Use the letters only once. There is one extra letter which you do not need to use.

A A good teacher praises effort.

Speaker 1 [ ] **19**

B A good teacher knows the subject well.

Speaker 2 [ ] **20**

C A good teacher is strict.

Speaker 3 [ ] **21**

D A good teacher is available outside the classroom.

Speaker 4 [ ] **22**

E A good teacher is entertaining.

Speaker 5 [ ] **23**

F A good teacher has experience.

Part 4

You will hear a radio interview about a mountain-climbing weekend. For questions **24–30**, choose the best answer (**A**, **B** or **C**).

---

24 How did Douglas feel when he booked the weekend?

   A   sure that he would enjoy training for it

   B   uncertain if it was a good idea for him

   C   surprised that such activities were organised

	24

25 Douglas expected that the experience would help him to

   A   meet people with similar interests.

   B   improve his physical fitness.

   C   discover his psychological limits.

	25

26 He was surprised that the other participants

   A   were there for reasons like his.

   B   were experienced climbers.

   C   were in better condition than him.

	26

27 What did one of his friends say to him?

   A   He was making a mistake.

   B   Climbing was fashionable.

   C   She was envious of him.

	27

28 What did the people plan at the end of the trip?

   A   to send each other postcards

   B   to take a different sort of trip together

   C   to go on another climbing trip together

	28

29 In what way did Douglas change as a result of the trip?

   A   He developed more interest in people.

   B   He became more ambitious.

   C   He began to notice more things around him.

	29

30 Douglas's boots are still muddy because he wants them to

   A   remind him of what he has achieved.

   B   warn him not to do it again.

   C   show other people what he has done.

	30

PAPER 5 SPEAKING (14 minutes)

You take the Speaking test with another candidate, referred to here as your partner. There are two examiners. One will speak to you and your partner and the other will be listening. Both examiners will award marks.

Part 1 (3 minutes)

The examiner asks you and your partner questions about yourselves. You may be asked about things like 'your home town', 'your interests', 'your career plans', etc.

Part 2 (4 minutes)

The examiner gives you two photographs and asks you to talk about them for one minute. The examiner then asks your partner a question about your photographs and your partner responds briefly.

Then the examiner gives your partner two different photographs. Your partner talks about these photographs for one minute. This time the examiner asks you a question about your partner's photographs and you respond briefly.

Part 3 (approximately 3 minutes)

The examiner asks you and your partner to talk together. You may be asked to solve a problem or try to come to a decision about something. For example, you might be asked to decide the best way to use some rooms in a language school. The examiner gives you a picture to help you but does not join in the conversation.

Part 4 (approximately 4 minutes)

The examiner joins in the conversation. You all talk together in a more general way about what has been said in Part 3. The examiner asks you questions but you and your partner are also expected to develop the conversation.

Test 3

PAPER 1 READING (1 hour 15 minutes)

Part 1

You are going to read a magazine article about the popularity of activity holidays. Choose the most suitable heading from the list **A–I** for each part (**1–7**) of the article. There is one extra heading which you do not need to use. There is an example at the beginning (**0**).

Mark your answers **on the separate answer sheet**.

A	A false sense of security
B	Remote destinations
C	Too risky for some
D	Holidays that don't quite work
E	New findings
F	Very little real danger
G	Too much routine
H	Second-hand experiences
I	Available to all

Activity Holidays

*Whether it's bungee-jumping, climbing or sky-diving, we want
to test ourselves on holiday. Peter Jones tries to find out why.*

0	I

Risk-taking for pleasure is on the increase. Adventure activities and 'extreme' sports are becoming very popular and attracting everyone from the young and fit to people who, until recently, were more likely to prefer walking round museums at weekends. Grandmothers are white-water rafting, secretaries are bungee-jumping, and accountants are climbing cliffs.

1	B

Well-planned summer expeditions to tropical locations are now fashionable for European university students. As they wander over ancient rocks or canoe past tiny villages, away from it all, it is quite possible to feel 'in tune with nature', a real explorer or adventurer.

2	F C

A whole branch of the travel industry is now developing around controlled risks. Ordinary trippers, too, are met off a plane, strapped into rafts or boats and are given the sort of adventure that they will remember for years. They pay their money and they trust their guides, and the wetter they get the better. Later, they buy the photograph of themselves 'risking all in the wild'.

3	B G

But why the fashion for taking risks, real or simulated? The point that most people make is that city life is tame, with little variety, and increasingly controlled. Physical exercise is usually restricted to aerobics in the gym on a Thursday, and a game of football or tennis in the park or a short walk at the weekend.

4	

Says Trish Malcolm, an independent tour operator: 'People want a sense of immediate achievement and the social element of shared physical experience is also important.' Other operators say that people find the usual type of breaks – such as a week on the beach – too slow. They say that participation in risk sports is a reflection of the restlessness in people. They are always on the go in their lives and want to keep up the momentum on holiday.

5	A

But psychologists think it's even deeper than this. Culturally, we are being separated from the physical, outside world. Recent research suggests that the average person spends less and less time out of doors per day.

6	C H

Nature and the great outdoors are mostly encountered through wildlife films or cinema, or seen rushing past the windows of a fast car. In a society where people are continually invited to watch rather than to participate, a two-hour ride down a wild and fast-flowing river can be incredibly exciting.

7	A

One psychologist believes that it is all part of our need to control nature. Because we have developed the technology to make unsinkable boats, boots that can stop us getting frostbite or jackets that allow us to survive in extreme temperatures, we are beginning to believe that nothing will harm us and that we are protected from nature. That is until nature shows us her true power in the form of a storm, flood or avalanche.

Part 2

You are going to read a magazine article in which a father describes his relationship with his son. For questions **8–14**, choose the answer (**A**, **B**, **C** or **D**) which you think fits best according to the text.

Mark your answers **on the separate answer sheet**.

Gary and Me

The restaurant owner John Moore writes about his relationship with his son Gary, the famous TV chef.

I believe everyone's given a chance in life. My son, Gary, was given his chance with cooking, and my chance was to run a restaurant. When I heard about the opportunity, I rushed over to look at the place. It was in a really bad state. It was perfect for what I had in mind.

Coming into this business made me recall my childhood. I can remember my mother going out to work in a factory and me being so upset because I was left alone. With that in mind, I thought, 'We want time for family life'. My wife dedicated herself to looking after the children and did all my accounts while I ran the business. We lived over the restaurant in those days, and we always put a lot of emphasis on having meals

line 16 together. It's paid dividends with our children, Gary and Joe. They're both very confident. Also, from a very early age they would come down and talk to our regular customers. It's given both of them a great start in life.

Gary was quite a lively child when he was really small. We had a corner bath, and when he was about seven he thought he'd jump into it like a swimming pool, and he knocked himself out. When he was older, he had to work for pocket money. He started off doing odd jobs and by the age of about ten he was in the kitchen every weekend, so he always had loads of money at school. He had discipline. He used to be up even before me in the morning. If you run a family business, it's for the family, and it was nice to see him helping out.

Gary wasn't very academic, but he shone so much in the kitchen. By the age of fifteen he was as good as any of the men working there, and sometimes he was even left in charge. He would

produce over a hundred meals, and from then I knew he'd go into catering because he had that flair. So when he came to me and said, 'Dad, I've got to do work experience as part of my course at school', I sent him to a friend of mine who's got a restaurant.

Gary recently took up playing the drums and now he has his own band. Goodness knows what will happen to the cooking if the music takes off. My advice to Gary would be: if you start chasing two hares, you end up catching neither, so chase the hare you know you're going to catch. He understood when I said to him: 'Gary, if you're going to get anywhere in life, you've got to do it by the age of 30. If you haven't done it by then, it's too late.' *line 52*

Gary went to catering college at the age of 17, and on his first day he and the other new students – they're normally complete beginners – were given what's supposed to be a morning's work. But within an hour, Gary had chopped all his vegetables, sliced all his meats. He'd prepared everything. That's my son for you! In the end, he was helping other people out.

None of us can believe how successful Gary's TV cookery series has become. I'm extremely proud of him. I've always tried to tell him that if you want something, you've got to work jolly hard for it, because no one gives you anything. He's seen the opportunity he's been given and grabbed hold of it with both hands. You know, you talk to your children as they grow up, and if they only take in ten per cent of what you've told them, you've got to be happy with that. The things Gary says, the things he does, I think, well, he must have listened sometimes.

8 How did the writer react to his own big chance?

    A He worried about the problems.
    B He saw what could be done.
    C He thought the family would suffer.
    D He wondered if he should take it.

9 How did the writer's childhood influence his own family life?

    A He realised that the pattern was repeating itself.
    B He encouraged his children to talk to him.
    C He made sure there was plenty of personal contact.
    D He forced his wife to stay at home.

10 What does the writer mean by 'paid dividends' in line 16?

    A brought financial reward
    B produced benefits
    C was worth the suffering
    D allowed money to be saved

11 As a young boy, Gary

    A showed how determined he could be.
    B was always in trouble.
    C was motivated by money.
    D demonstrated a variety of talents.

12 What does 'done it' refer to in line 52?

    A chosen a profession
    B achieved success
    C caught a hare
    D lived your life

13 According to his father, what was typical about Gary's behaviour on his first day at college?

    A He helped other people.
    B He impressed those in charge.
    C He tried to make his father proud.
    D He performed the task efficiently.

14 How does his father regard Gary's upbringing?

    A His encouragement has caused Gary's success.
    B The family influence on Gary was too strong.
    C Gary has forgotten important lessons.
    D Gary has learnt some essential things.

Part 3

You are going to read a magazine article about learning to fly a plane. Eight paragraphs have been removed from the article. Choose from the paragraphs **A–I** the one which fits each gap (**15–21**). There is one extra paragraph which you do not need to use. There is an example at the beginning (**0**).

Mark your answers **on the separate answer sheet**.

Learning to Fly

I had been testing cars and motorcycles for over twenty years. I couldn't take any more. It wasn't terribly exciting and, in any case, new cars were beginning to look identical and drive similarly. What I needed was a new challenge.

0	I

Unfortunately, I wore glasses. The Royal Air Force wouldn't consider anyone for pilot training unless they had perfect eyesight. Halfway through an aptitude test, they realised that my eyes were far from perfect. I didn't stand a chance.

15	

It was an obvious choice. It's just twenty minutes' drive from my home. It's very quiet, too, so the £90 per hour for the training is spent flying in the air, not waiting on the ground for other planes to take off.

16	

It took me a whole year to get my private pilot's licence. It started well, with my first solo flight coming after just seven hours. Then came all the studying, the exams, the hard work. I never thought I'd get to the end of it.

17	

Then came last winter and the end of the course was in sight. For weeks, the weather was so terrible that for most of the time it was impossible to fly. Strong winds, heavy rain and even snow and ice made flying conditions extremely hazardous.

18	

But finally the first of three practical exams arrived – the navigation test. The examiner sets you a course that you have to plan according to the weather, and then fly with him sitting beside you.

19	

I passed this test, but I don't know how. The second test involves flying cross-country to two other airports, which you can choose, and landing at both. The important thing is to give the right messages to the air-traffic control people and understand their replies.

20	

After this alarming episode, the exercises in the flight-handling test were simple. As we completed the sixth exercise, the examiner suddenly turned to me and said, 'Congratulations – you've passed!'

21	

I wasn't sure why, because we usually land as slowly as possible. Then I turned round and realised straightaway: we were being followed by a British Airways jumbo jet!

A A week which I had set aside for finishing the course came and went with no possibility of getting in the air at all. And besides the problems with the weather, my second son was born, and that made it even more difficult to find the time for lessons and studying.

B But the real reason I chose this club was that a friend of mine, Andrew Wilkins, is the chief instructor there. He impressed me by taking me out for a free flight just so that I could see what it was like.

C Unfortunately, I got myself lost this time and flew too far east. I completely missed the first airport. However, I flew over a car factory I recognised and managed to get back on course.

D Along the way, he'll take the controls and fly off course, just to get you lost. Then he'll hand back the controls to you and expect you to find your way home.

E One day I was asked by an air-traffic controller if I could see another aircraft ahead. I said yes, and immediately it disappeared into a cloud. I just didn't know what to do.

F At the time, taking private lessons to learn how to fly was financially beyond me. So I had to delay my plans to become a pilot for quite a while. It was twenty years, in fact, before I finally enrolled at a flying club in Hertfordshire.

G Since getting my pilot's licence, I've been out flying a few times. The highlight so far was flying up to Birmingham International Airport for a motor show with Andrew beside me. As we approached the runway, the air-traffic controller came on the radio asking for as much speed as our little plane could manage.

H For months, my head was always in a book and my head hurt from all the facts, figures and flying instructions.

I This feeling of needing a change coincided with my 40th birthday, which started me thinking about what I'd been doing all those years. When I left school all I had really wanted to do was fly.

Part 4

You are going to read an article about the effect of advertising on children. For questions **22–35**, choose from the sections of the article (**A–F**). The sections may be chosen more than once. There is an example at the beginning (**0**).

Mark your answers **on the separate answer sheet**.

Which section of the article mentions

the kind of shop in which TV advertising expects to see results?	**0**	**B**
the influence a parent has had over their child's views?	**22**	
the fact that children do not understand why their parents refuse their demands?	**23**	
a parent who understands why children make demands?	**24**	
a family who rarely argue while shopping?	**25**	
someone who feels children ought to find out for themselves how to make decisions about what to buy?	**26**	
the fact that parents can be mistaken about what food is good for you?	**27**	
an unexpected benefit for shops?	**28**	
a parent who regrets buying what their children have asked for?	**29**	
a parent who has different rules for themselves and their children?	**30**	
a parent who feels annoyed even before the children ask for anything?	**31**	
the fact that parents blame the advertisers for the difficult situation they find themselves in?	**32**	
the regularity of children's demands?	**33**	
the need for parents to discuss food with their children?	**34**	
a TV advertising rule which has little effect?	**35**	

Young Shoppers

A Supermarket shopping with children, one mother says, is absolute murder: 'They want everything they see. If it's not the latest sugar-coated breakfast cereal, it's a Disney video or a comic. Usually all three. I can't afford all this stuff and, anyway, if I agree to their demands I feel I've been persuaded against my better judgement and I feel guilty about buying and feeding them rubbish. Yet I hate myself for saying no all the time, and I get cross and defensive in anticipation as we leave home. I do my best to avoid taking them shopping but then I worry that I'm not allowing them to have the experience they need in order to make their own choices. I can't win.'

B Research has found that children taken on a supermarket trip make a purchase request every two minutes. More than £150 million a year is now spent on advertising directly to children, most of it on television. That figure is likely to increase and it is in the supermarket aisles that the investment is most likely to be successful. For children, the reasons behind their parents' decisions about what they can and cannot afford are often unclear, and arguments about how bad sugar is for your teeth are unconvincing when compared with the attractive and emotionally persuasive advertising campaigns.

C According to Susan Dibb of the National Food Alliance, 'Most parents are concerned about what they give their children to eat and have ideas about what food is healthy – although those ideas are not always accurate. Obviously, such a dialogue between parents and children is a good thing, because if the only information children are getting about products is from TV advertising, they are getting a very one-sided view. Parents resent the fact that they are competing with the advertising industry and are forced into the position of repeatedly disappointing their children.' The Independent Television Commission, which regulates TV advertising, prohibits advertisers from telling children to ask their parents to buy products. But, as Dibb points out, 'The whole purpose of advertising is to persuade the viewer to buy something. So even if they cannot say, "Tell your mum to buy this product," the intended effect is precisely that.'

D A major source of stress for some parents shopping with children is the mental energy required to decide which demands should be agreed to and which should be refused. One mother says she has patience when it comes to discussing food with her children, but she still feels unhappy about the way she manages their shopping demands: 'My son does pay attention to advertisements but he is critical of them. We talk a lot about different products and spend time looking at labels. I've talked about it so much that I've brainwashed him into thinking all adverts are rubbish. We have very little conflict in the supermarket now because the children don't ask for things I won't want to buy.'

E Parents also admit they are inconsistent, even hypocritical, in their responses to their children's purchasing requests. Mike, father of a son of seven and a daughter of three, says, 'We refuse to buy him the sweets he wants on the grounds that it's bad for him while we are busy loading the trolley with double cream and chocolate for ourselves. It's enjoyable to buy nice things, and it's quite reasonable that children should want to share that, I suppose. But I still find myself being irritated by their demands. It partly depends on how I feel. If I'm feeling generous and things are going well in my life, I'm more likely to say yes. It's hard to be consistent.'

F Supermarkets themselves could do a lot more to <u>ease</u> parent-child conflict by removing sweets from checkout areas or even by providing supervised play areas. Although parents might spend less without their children with them, the thought of shopping without your six-year-old's demands would surely attract enough extra customers to more than make up the difference.

PAPER 2   WRITING (1 hour 30 minutes)

Part 1

You **must** answer this question.

---

1   An English friend, Sam, visited you recently and has just sent you a letter and some photographs. Read Sam's letter and the notes you have made on it. Then write a suitable letter to Sam, using all your notes.

Thanks for taking me to the airport. I hope your journey home wasn't too long.

Over 3 hours because …

I really enjoyed staying with you. Here are the photos I took. I'm sure you'd like extra copies. Could you tell me which photos you'd like?

Describe the ones I want.

When I got home, I realised I had left my watch behind. It's green and gold. You haven't found it, have you?

I have! Explain where.

I think we'll have a great time together when you come here in September. We could either spend the whole time here in the city or in the countryside on my uncle's farm. Which would you like to do?

Send watch now or …?

Say which and why.

Write a **letter** of between **120** and **180** words in an appropriate style.
Do not write any postal addresses.

Part 2

Write an answer to **one** of the questions 2–5 in this part. Write your answer in **120–180** words in an appropriate style.

---

2   Your teacher has asked you to write a composition, giving your opinions on the following statement:

Your teenage years are the best years of your life!

Write your **composition**.

3   You see the following notice in an international magazine.

Be someone famous for a day

If you could change places for 24 hours with a famous person alive today, who would you choose, and why?

The best article will be published in our magazine next month.

Write your **article**.

4   You have decided to enter a short story competition in an international magazine. The competition rules say that the story must **end** with the following words:

That one telephone call changed my life for ever.

Write your **story**.

5   Answer **one** of the following two questions based on your reading of **one** of these set books. Write **(a)** or **(b)** as well as the number **5** in the question box, and the **title** of the book next to the box. Your answer **must** be about one of the books below.

Best Detective Stories of Agatha Christie – Longman Fiction
A Tale of Two Cities – Charles Dickens
Animal Farm – George Orwell
More Tales from Shakespeare – Charles and Mary Lamb
Round the World in Eighty Days – Jules Verne

Either   **(a)**   In the story you have read, which character would you most like to be? Write a **composition** for your teacher, answering this question with reference to the book or one of the short stories you have read.

Or   **(b)**   'A love story is an essential part of every good book.' Do you agree or disagree with this statement? Write a **composition**, giving your opinions with reference to the book or one of the short stories you have read.

PAPER 3   USE OF ENGLISH (1 hour 15 minutes)

Part 1

For questions **1–15**, read the text below and decide which answer (**A**, **B**, **C** or **D**) best fits each space. There is an example at the beginning (**0**).

Mark your answers **on the separate answer sheet.**

Example:

0   **A** catch   **B** pick   **C** find   **D** gain

0	A	B	C	D
	▬	▭	▭	▭

A GOOD START TO A HOLIDAY

I had never been to Denmark before, so when I set out to **(0)** ..... the ferry in early May, I little **(1)** ..... that by the end of the trip I'd have made such lasting friendships.

Esjberg is a **(2)** ..... port for a cyclist's arrival, where tourist information can be **(3)** ..... and money changed. A cycle track **(4)** ..... out of town and down to Ribe, where I spent my first night. The only appointment I had to **(5)** ..... was a meeting with a friend who was flying out in June. I wanted to **(6)** ..... my time well, so I had planned a route which would **(7)** ..... several small islands and various **(8)** ..... of the countryside.

In my **(9)** ..... , a person travelling alone sometimes meets with unexpected hospitality, and this trip was no **(10)** ..... . On only my second day, I got into conversation with a cheerful man who turned **(11)** ..... to be the local baker. He insisted that I should **(12)** ..... his family for lunch, and, while we were eating, he contacted his daughter in Odense. Within minutes, he had **(13)** ..... for me to visit her and her family. Then I was **(14)** ..... on my way with a fresh loaf of bread to keep me **(15)** ..... , and the feeling that this would turn out to be a wonderful holiday.

1 **A** wondered   **B** suspected   **C** doubted   **D** judged

2 **A** capable   **B** ready   **C** favourable   **D** convenient

3 **A** met   **B** united   **C** established   **D** obtained

4 **A** leads   **B** rides   **C** moves   **D** connects

5 **A** do   **B** support   **C** keep   **D** maintain

6 **A** take   **B** serve   **C** exercise   **D** use

7 **A** include   **B** contain   **C** enclose   **D** consist

8 **A** sectors   **B** parts   **C** zones   **D** places

9 **A** experience   **B** knowledge   **C** observation   **D** information

10 **A** difference   **B** change   **C** exception   **D** contrast

11 **A** up   **B** out   **C** in   **D** over

12 **A** greet   **B** see   **C** join   **D** approach

13 **A** arranged   **B** fixed   **C** settled   **D** ordered

14 **A** passed   **B** sent   **C** begun   **D** put

15 **A** doing   **B** making   **C** being   **D** going

Part 2

For questions **16–30**, read the text below and think of the word which best fits each space. Use only **one** word in each space. There is an example at the beginning (**0**).

Write your answers **on the separate answer sheet**.

Example: | 0 | *away* |

DEALING WITH WASTE PLASTIC

Every year people throw (**0**) ...*away*... millions of tonnes of plastic bottles, boxes and wrapping. These create huge mountains of waste (**16**) .... are extremely hard to get (**17**) .... of. Now, a new recycling process promises to reduce this problem by turning old plastic (**18**) .... new.

Scientists have taken (**19**) .... long time to develop their ideas because waste plastic has always been a bigger problem (**20**) .... substances like waste paper. You can bury plastic, but it is years (**21**) .... it breaks down. If you burn it, it just becomes another form of pollution. A (**22**) .... products, for example bottles, can be re-used but it is expensive or difficult to do this (**23**) .... a lot of plastic products.

Now a group of companies has developed a new method (**24**) .... recycling that could save almost (**25**) .... plastic waste. The advantage of the new process is that nearly every type of waste plastic can be used: it does (**26**) .... have to be sorted. In addition, labels and ink may be left (**27**) .... the products. Everything is simply mixed together (**28**) .... heated to more than 400 degrees centigrade (**29**) .... that it melts. It is then cooled, producing a waxy substance that can be used to make new plastic products such as bags, bottles and, among (**30**) .... things, computer hardware.

Part 3

For questions **31–40**, complete the second sentence so that it has a similar meaning to the first sentence, using the word given. **Do not change the word given.** You must use between **two** and **five** words, including the word given.

Here is an example (**0**).

Example:

0 You must do exactly what the manager tells you.

carry

You must .... instructions exactly.

The space can be filled by the words 'carry out the manager's' so you write:

0	*carry out the manager's*

Write **only** the missing words on **the separate answer sheet**.

---

31 The teacher postponed the theatre trip until the summer term.

off

The theatre trip .... the teacher until the summer term.

32 'What is the width of this cupboard?' Rebecca asked her sister.

wide

Rebecca asked her sister .... was.

33 George spent ages tidying up his room.

took

It .... up his room.

34 Claire accidentally damaged my book.

mean

Claire .... my book.

35 A famous architect designed Dr Schneider's house for her.

had

Dr Schneider .... a famous architect.

36 'Peter, you've eaten all the ice-cream!' said his mother.

accused

Peter's mother .... all the ice-cream.

37 Jim fell off his bike because he wasn't looking where he was going.

paying

If Jim .... to where he was going, he wouldn't have fallen off his bike.

38 Maria apologised for breaking Sarah's camera.

sorry

Maria said she .... broken Sarah's camera.

39 We might not find it easy to book a seat at the last minute.

could

It .... us to book a seat at the last minute.

40 It was wrong of you to borrow my jacket without asking.

ought

You .... before you borrowed my jacket.

Part 4

For questions **41–55**, read the text below and look carefully at each line. Some of the lines are correct, and some have a word which should not be there.

If a line is correct, put a tick (✓) by the number **on the separate answer sheet**. If a line has a word which should **not** be there, write the word **on the separate answer sheet**. There are two examples at the beginning (**0** and **00**).

0	✓

Examples:

00	*with*

THE PAINTING

0	In the village where I grew up, everyone knew an old man
00	who spent all of his time with painting. People who lived in the
41	village used to be admire his work and he often gave paintings
42	to friends of his. If they offered him money, he would never
43	take it because he said he painted for a pleasure. He gave one of
44	the paintings to my father, who actually wasn't very interested
45	in art. One day when I was playing, I came across from it in the
46	bin outside our house. I have hid it in our garage where my father
47	couldn't find it because I really would liked it, and then I forgot
48	all about it. Since years later I found it again. By that time the
49	old man had been died and people had started to recognise his
50	paintings as great works of art. They were now worth a lot of
51	money. An art gallery made me an offer of £5,000 for this
52	painting and I nearly sold it, but then I decided not to do. When
53	I look at the painting held hanging on the wall of my sitting-room,
54	it reminds to me of my childhood, and of the man who could
55	have been so much rich but didn't really want to make money.

Part 5

For questions **56–65**, read the text below. Use the word given in capitals at the end of each line to form a word that fits in the space in the **same** line. There is an example at the beginning (**0**).

Write your answers **on the separate answer sheet**.

Example:

0	*cheerfully*

AN UNUSUAL SWIMMING CLUB

Members of a special club in Britain **(0)** ...*cheerfully*... leave the warmth	**CHEER**
of their beds, while most sensible people are still fast **(56)** .... , for	**SLEEP**
an **(57)** .... swim in water with a temperature of only seven degrees	**ENERGY**
centigrade. This may sound like **(58)** .... to you, but these swimmers	**MAD**
firmly believe that it is **(59)** .... to do this, even in mid-winter.	**HEALTH**
(60) .... of the club requires daily swimming outdoors. However,	**MEMBER**
for people not used to large **(61)** .... in temperature,	**DIFFERENT**
it may not be such a good idea. While there is an **(62)** .... in	**IMPROVE**
the blood circulation of people who swim **(63)** .... in icy water,	**REGULAR**
it can be **(64)** .... to others. But when members are asked why they	**HARM**
do it, the common **(65)** .... is that it makes them feel wonderful!	**RESPOND**

PAPER 4   LISTENING (approximately 40 minutes)

Part 1

You will hear people talking in eight different situations. For questions **1–8**, choose the best answer (**A**, **B** or **C**).

---

1   You hear a man talking to a group of people who are going on an expedition into the rainforest.
What does he advise them against?

    A   sleeping in places where insects are found

    B   using substances which attract insects

    C   bathing in areas where insects are common

2   You overhear two people talking about a school football competition.
What did the woman think of the event?

    A   She didn't think anyone had enjoyed it.

    B   It managed to fulfil its aims.

    C   Not enough people had helped to set it up.

3   You hear a woman talking about her studies at the Beijing Opera School.
How did she feel when she first started her classes?

    A   worried about being much older than the other students

    B   disappointed because her dictionary was unhelpful

    C   annoyed by the lack of communication with her teacher

4   You hear a famous comedian talking on the radio about his early career.
Why is he telling this story?

    A   to show how lucky he was at the beginning

    B   to show the value of a good course

    C   to show that he has always been a good comedian

5 You hear someone talking on the phone.
   Who is she talking to?

   A someone at her office

   B someone at a travel information centre

   C a family member

6 You hear a novelist talking about how she writes.
   How does she get her ideas for her novels?

   A She bases her novels on personal experiences.

   B Ideas come to her once she starts writing.

   C She lets ideas develop gradually in her mind.

7 You hear a woman talking to a friend on the phone.
   What is she doing?

   A refusing an invitation

   B denying an accusation

   C apologising for a mistake

8 You hear a radio announcement about a future programme.
   What kind of programme is it?

   A a play about a child

   B a reading from a children's book

   C a holiday programme

Part 2

You will hear an interview with a man who enjoys flying in a small aircraft called a 'microlight'. For questions **9–18**, complete the sentences.

Before his retirement, Brian worked as a pilot for a company called

	9

for a long time.

Brian feels like a bird when flying his microlight because he doesn't have a

	10

around him.

Brian disagrees with the suggestion that steering a microlight is like steering a

	11

Brian's record-breaking flight ended in

	12

Brian organised his flight in advance to avoid needing other people as

	13

on the way.

Brian's microlight was modified so that it could carry more

	14

on board.

It took Brian

	15

to plan the record-breaking flight.

Brian feels that flying over miles and miles of

	16

was the most dangerous part of the trip.

Brian describes his navigation system as both

	17

and easy to use.

Brian says that his main problem on the flight was the fact that he became very

	18

Part 3

You will hear five different people talking about short courses they have attended. For questions **19–23**, choose from the list (**A–F**) what each speaker says about their course. Use the letters only once. There is one extra letter which you do not need to use.

A I was encouraged by the teachers to continue developing my skill.

B I learnt something about the subject that I hadn't expected.

C I preferred the social life to the course content.

D I intend doing a similar course again.

E I found out something about myself.

F I thought the course was good value for money.

Speaker 1	19
Speaker 2	20
Speaker 3	21
Speaker 4	22
Speaker 5	23

Part 4

You will hear part of a radio interview with Martin Middleton, who makes wildlife programmes for television. For questions **24–30**, choose the best answer (**A**, **B** or **C**).

24 What was the origin of Martin Middleton's love of travel?

    A   living abroad in the 1960s

    B   something he read as a child

    C   a television film about Africa

                                   24

25 When he visited Borneo, Martin

    A   had no fixed expectations.

    B   made a programme about life on the river.

    C   became more interested in filming old buildings.

                                   25

26 Since the early 1960s, wildlife filming has become

    A   more relaxed.

    B   more creative.

    C   more organised.

                                   26

27 Looking back, Martin regards his experience on the iceberg as

    A   slightly ridiculous.

    B   extremely dangerous.

    C   strangely depressing.

                                   27

28 When he takes a holiday, Martin prefers to

    A   relax by the sea.

    B   stay in comfortable surroundings.

    C   travel for a particular reason.

                                   28

29 Martin thought that the holiday-makers he saw in the Dominican Republic were

    A   risking their health.

    B   wasting opportunities.

    C   lacking entertainment.

                                   29

30 What is Martin's opinion of tourism?

    A   It should be discouraged.

    B   It can be a good thing.

    C   It is well managed.

                                   30

PAPER 5   SPEAKING (14 minutes)

You take the Speaking test with another candidate, referred to here as your partner. There are two examiners. One will speak to you and your partner and the other will be listening. Both examiners will award marks.

Part 1 (3 minutes)

The examiner asks you and your partner questions about yourselves. You may be asked about things like 'your home town', 'your interests', 'your career plans', etc.

Part 2 (4 minutes)

The examiner gives you two photographs and asks you to talk about them for one minute. The examiner then asks your partner a question about your photographs and your partner responds briefly.

Then the examiner gives your partner two different photographs. Your partner talks about these photographs for one minute. This time the examiner asks you a question about your partner's photographs and you respond briefly.

Part 3 (approximately 3 minutes)

The examiner asks you and your partner to talk together. You may be asked to solve a problem or try to come to a decision about something. For example, you might be asked to decide the best way to use some rooms in a language school. The examiner gives you a picture to help you but does not join in the conversation.

Part 4 (approximately 4 minutes)

The examiner joins in the conversation. You all talk together in a more general way about what has been said in Part 3. The examiner asks you questions but you and your partner are also expected to develop the conversation.

Test 4

PAPER 1   READING (1 hour 15 minutes)

Part 1

You are going to read a magazine article about a man who teaches children how to improve their memory. Choose the most suitable heading from the list **A–I** for each part (**1–7**) of the article. There is one extra heading which you do not need to use. There is an example at the beginning (**0**).

Mark your answers **on the separate answer sheet**.

A	An obvious need
B	Gaining attention
C	The odder the better
D	Making sense of information
E	Trade secrets
F	Academic approval
G	A change of focus
H	Selected memories
I	An ancient skill

Memory test

Jerome Burne talks to a magician who teaches children ways to remember facts.

0   I

The Greek philosophers knew about it and it could still dramatically improve children's school results today, except that no one teaches it. 'It' is a very old technique for making your memory better. Try memorising this series of random numbers: 3,6,5,5,2,1,2,4. About as meaningful as dates in history or equations in maths, aren't they? Chances are you won't remember them in five minutes, let alone in five hours. However, had you been at a lecture given at a school in the south of England last month, you would now be able to fix them in your head for five days, five weeks, in fact for ever.

1

'I am going to give you five techniques that will enable you to remember anything you need to know at school,' promised lecturer Ian Robinson to a fascinated audience of a hundred schoolchildren. He slapped his hand down on the table. In his other life, Robinson is an entertainer, and he was using all the tricks he had picked up in his career. 'When I've finished in two hours' time, your work will be far more effective and productive. Anyone not interested, leave now.' The entire room sat still, glued to their seats.

2

When he entertains, Robinson calls himself the Mind Magician. He specialises in doing magic tricks that look totally impossible, and then he reveals that they involve nothing more mysterious than good old-fashioned trickery. 'I have always been interested in tricks involving memory – being able to reel off the order of cards in a pack, that sort of thing,' he explains.

3

Robinson was already lecturing to schools on his magic techniques when it struck him that students might find memory techniques even more valuable. 'It wasn't a difficult area to move into, as the stuff's all there in books.' So he summarised everything to make a two-hour lecture about five techniques.

4

What Robinson's schoolchildren get are methods that will be familiar to anyone who has dipped into any one of a dozen books on memory. The difference is that Robinson's approach is firmly aimed at schoolchildren. The basic idea is to take material that is random and meaningless – musical scales, the bones of the arm – and give them a structure. That series of numbers at the beginning of the article fits in here. Once you think of it as the number of days in the year – 365 – and the number of weeks – 52 – and so on, it suddenly becomes permanently memorable.

5

'You want to learn a list of a hundred things? A thousand? No problem,' says Robinson. The scandal is that every child is not taught the techniques from the beginning of their school life. The schoolchildren who were watching him thought it was brilliant. 'I wish I'd been told this earlier,' commented Mark, after Robinson had shown them how to construct 'mental journeys'.

6

Essentially, you visualise a walk down a street, or a trip round a room, and pick the points where you will put the things you want to remember – the lamppost, the fruit bowl. Then in each location you put a visual representation of your list – phrasal verbs, historical dates, whatever – making them as strange as possible. It is that simple, and it works.

7

The reaction of schools has been uniformly enthusiastic. 'The pupils benefited enormously from Ian's presentation,' says Dr Johnston, head of the school where Robinson was speaking. 'Ideally we should run a regular class in memory techniques so pupils can pick it up gradually.'

Part 2

You are going to read an article about the actress Harriet Walter. For questions **8–15**, choose the answer (**A, B, C** or **D**) which you think fits best according to the text.

Mark your answers **on the separate answer sheet**.

Acting minus the drama

Harriet Walter has written a fascinating book about her profession.
Benedicte Page reports.

It is not often that an experienced actor with a high public profile will sit down to answer in depth the ordinary theatregoer's questions: how do you put together a character which isn't your own?; what is it like to perform the same play night after night?; or simply, why do you do it? Harriet Walter was prompted to write *Other People's Shoes: Thoughts on Acting* by a sense that many people's interest in theatre extended beyond the scope of entertainment chit-chat. 'I was asked very intelligent, probing questions by people who weren't in the profession, from taxi drivers to dinner-party hosts to people in shopping queues. It made me realise that people have an interest in what we do which goes beyond show-business gossip,' she says.

Other People's Shoes avoids insider gossip and, mostly, autobiography: 'If events in my life had had a huge direct influence, I would have put them in, but they didn't,' Harriet says, though she does explain how her parents' divorce was a factor in her career. But the focus of the book is to share – remarkably openly – the inside experience of the stage and the rehearsal room, aiming to replace the false sense of mystery with a more realistic understanding and respect for the profession.

'There's a certain double edge to the publicity an actor can get in the newspapers: it gives you attention but, by giving it to you, simultaneously criticises you,' Harriet says. 'People ask you to talk about yourself and then say, "Oh, actors are so self-centred." And the "sound-bite" variety of journalism, which touches on many things but never allows you to go into them in depth, leaves you with a sort of shorthand which reinforces prejudices and myths.'

Harriet's career began in the 1970s and has included theatre performances with the Royal Shakespeare Company and television and film roles. She writes wittily about the embarrassments of the rehearsal room, as actors try out their half-formed ideas. And she is at pains to demystify the theatre: the question 'How do you do the same play every night?' is answered by a simple comparison with the familiar car journey you take every day, which presents a slightly different challenge each time. 'I was trying to get everyone to understand that this extraordinary mystery and you're not visited by some spiritual inspiration every night.'

line 54

Harriet's own acting style is to build up a character piece by piece. She says that this process is not widely understood: 'There's no intelligent vocabulary out there for discussing the craft of building characters. Reviews of an actor's performance which appear in the newspapers are generally based on whether the reviewer likes the actors or not. It's not about whether they are being skilful or not, or how intelligent their choices are.'

There remains something mysterious about slipping into 'other people's shoes': 'It's something like falling in love,' Harriet says. 'When you're in love with someone, you go in and out of separateness and togetherness. It's similar with acting and you can slip in and out of a character. Once a character has been built, it remains with you, at the end of a phone line, as it were, waiting for your call.'

Harriet includes her early work in *Other People's Shoes* – 'I wanted to separate myself from those who say, "What an idiot I was, what a load of nonsense we all talked in those days!"; it wasn't all rubbish, and it has affected how I approach my work and my audiences.' And she retains from those days her belief in the vital role of the theatre.

8 Harriet Walter decided to write her book because she

   A was tired of answering people's questions about acting.
   B knew people liked to read about showbusiness gossip.
   C wanted to entertain people through her writing.
   D wanted to satisfy people's curiosity about acting in the theatre.

9 In paragraph two, we learn that Harriet's book aims to

   A correct some of the impressions people have of the theatre.
   B relate important details about her own life story.
   C analyse the difficulties of a career in the theatre.
   D tell the truth about some of the actors she has worked with.

10 What problem do actors have with newspaper publicity?

   A It never focuses on the actors who deserve it.
   B It often does more harm than good.
   C It never reports what actors have actually said.
   D It often makes mistakes when reporting facts.

11 Harriet uses the example of the car journey to show that

   A acting can be boring as well as rewarding.
   B actors do not find it easy to try new ideas.
   C actors do not deserve the praise they receive.
   D acting shares characteristics with other repetitive activities.

12 What does 'it' refer to in line 54?

   A facing a different challenge
   B taking a familiar car journey
   C acting in the same play every night
   D working with fellow actors

13 Harriet criticises theatre reviewers because they

   A do not give enough recognition to the art of character acting.
   B do not realise that some parts are more difficult to act than others.
   C choose the wrong kinds of plays to review.
   D suggest that certain actors have an easy job.

14 Harriet says that after actors have played a particular character, they

   A may be asked to play other similar characters.
   B may become a bit like the character.
   C will never want to play the part again.
   D will never forget how to play the part.

15 What does Harriet say about her early work?

   A It has been a valuable influence on the work she has done since.
   B It was completely different from the kind of work she does now.
   C She finds it embarrassing to recall that period of her life.
   D She is annoyed when people criticise the work she did then.

Part 3

You are going to read a newspaper article about a man who is running round the world. Eight paragraphs have been removed from the article. Choose from the paragraphs **A–I** the one which fits each gap (**16–22**). There is one extra paragraph which you do not need to use. There is an example at the beginning (**0**).

Mark your answers **on the separate answer sheet**.

The Runningman

Bryan Green, a 32-year-old from London, calls himself the 'Runningman'. He runs and keeps on running through towns, cities, up mountains and across rivers. Green has set his sights on running round the world.

| **0** | **I** |

He then flew to the north of Japan and ran to Osaka in the south. In Australia he ran from Perth to Sydney, and then he began in the Americas, bringing his current total to 23 countries, 45,000 kilometres and 30 pairs of trainers.

| **16** | |

When I met Green in Rio, he had just run 70 kilometres, his daily average. He was holding in one hand a two-litre bottle of fizzy juice and in the other a piece of paper that he needed someone to sign, to confirm the time at which he had arrived.

| **17** | |

He travels light, carrying with him less than many people take to work. In his backpack he has a palmtop computer, a digital video camera, a Nikon 35mm camera, a map, a toothbrush and one change of clothes.

| **18** | |

'The original idea was just to see the world,' he told me. 'But, as I soon realised, I could make myself a future. I have learnt how to make money out of what I do.' He started off with £20 in his pocket and estimates that he has earned about £60,000 so far.

| **19** | |

And there is something of the explorer about him. 'Of course, I've found some places easier than others,' he says.

| **20** | |

At one point on that stage of the journey, Green got lost and was unable to find enough to eat. But generally he has been lucky with his health: he has not been injured and has never fallen ill.

| **21** | |

He speaks no language apart from English and, with no space for a dictionary, has a plastic-covered sheet of A4 paper with a dozen useful phrases in various languages. Over dinner he is keen to talk about the Amazon jungle.

| **22** | |

However, perhaps the point of a run like Green's is not to indulge in proper preparation. Its beauty is in the improvisation. 'I don't really analyse the run any more, I just do it,' he says.

A I did it for him. Even though he already holds the world long-distance running record, he still needs to continue proving he is keeping up a reasonable running speed.

B He has not yet sorted out a route and appears surprised when I tell him that there are no proper roads across it, as local people prefer to use the rivers instead.

C He's done this by selling his story to journalists. He is very aware that he is a marketable product.

D He has learned that you must take only what you will use. He has no medical supplies and no proper waterproofs.

E Apart from the day in south Australia where it was 45 °C in the shade and he collapsed, Australia is, he says, perfect running country. This compares to his experiences in temperatures of –30 °C in parts of Asia.

F Next week he heads off north, towards the Amazon, hoping to run to New York. After that, he just has to take care of Africa and Antarctica.

G So he is a touchingly solitary figure. He is too mobile to be able to make many friends, although he did meet someone in Australia who cycled next to him for 600 kilometres.

H Fortunately, the cold and the rain don't seem to bother him. It is partly his strength of character that made him refuse to take health insurance.

I The Runningman recently arrived in Rio de Janeiro in Brazil via a roundabout route: he left London four years ago and ran through Europe to China.

Part 4

You are going to read an article about people who changed their jobs. For questions **23–35**, choose from the people (**A–D**). The people may be chosen more than once. There is an example at the beginning (**0**).

Mark your answers **on the separate answer sheet**.

Which person mentions

enjoying their pastime more than the job they used to do?	**0**	**B**
enjoying being in charge of their own life?	**23**	
being surprised by suddenly losing their previous job?	**24**	
not having other people depending on them financially?	**25**	
missing working with other people?	**26**	
undergoing training in order to take up their new job?	**27**	
a contact being useful in promoting their new business?	**28**	
not being interested in possible promotion in their old job?	**29**	
disliking the amount of time they used to have to work?	**30**	
surprising someone else by the decision they made?	**31**	
a prediction that hasn't come true?	**32**	
consulting other people about their businesses?	**33**	
the similarities between their new job and their old one?	**34**	
working to a strict timetable?	**35**	

A NEW LIFE

A The Farmer

Matt Froggatt used to be an insurance agent in the City of London but now runs a sheep farm.

'After 14 years in business, I found that the City had gone from a place which was exciting to work in to a grind – no one was having fun any more. But I hadn't planned to leave for another five or ten years when I was made redundant. It came out of the blue, but it made me take a careful look at my life. I didn't get a particularly good pay-off but it was enough to set up the farm with. My break came when I got to know the head chef of a local hotel with one of the top 20 hotel restaurants in the country. Through supplying them, my reputation spread and now I also supply meat through mail order. I'm glad I'm no longer stuck in the office but it's astonishing how little things have changed for me: the same 80- to 90-hour week and still selling a product.'

B The Painter

Ron Ablewhite was a manager in advertising but now makes a living as an artist.

'My painting began as a hobby but I realised I was getting far more excitement out of it than out of working. The decision to take redundancy and to become an artist seemed logical. The career counsellor I talked to was very helpful. I think I was the first person who had ever told him, "I don't want to go back to where I've been." He was astonished because the majority of people in their mid-forties need to get back to work immediately – they need the money. But we had married young and our children didn't need our support. It was a leap into the unknown. We went to the north of England, where we didn't know a soul. It meant leaving all our friends, but we've been lucky in that our friendships have survived the distance – plenty of them come up and visit us now.'

C The Hatmaker

After working for five years as a company lawyer, Katherine Goodison set up her own business in her London flat, making hats for private clients.

'My job as a lawyer was fun. It was stimulating and I earned a lot of money, but the hours were terrible. I realised I didn't want to become a senior partner in the company, working more and more hours, so I left. A lot of people said I'd get bored, but that has never happened. The secret is to have deadlines. Since it's a fashion-related business, you have the collections, next year's shapes, the season – there's always too much to do, so you have to run a very regimented diary. I feel happier now, and definitely less stressed. There are things I really long for, though, like the social interaction with colleagues. What I love about this job is that I'm totally responsible for the product. If I do a rubbish job, then I'm the one who takes the blame. Of course, you care when you're working for a company, but when your name is all over the promotional material, you care that little bit more.'

D The Masseur

Paul Drinkwater worked in finance for 16 years before becoming a masseur at the Life Centre in London.

'I had been in financial markets from the age of 22, setting up deals. I liked the adrenaline but I never found the work rewarding. I was nearly made redundant in 1989, but I escaped by resigning and travelling for a year. I spent that year trying to work out what I wanted to do. I was interested in health, so I visited some of the world's best gymnasiums and talked to the owners about how they started up. I knew that to change career I had to get qualifications so I did various courses in massage. Then I was offered part-time work at the Life Centre. I have no regrets. I never used to feel in control, but now I have peace of mind and control of my destiny. That's best of all.'

PAPER 2   WRITING (1 hour 30 minutes)

Part 1

You **must** answer this question.

1   Your English friend, Kim, has written to you asking you if you'd like to go to a concert by your favourite band, Red Stone.

Read Kim's letter, on which you have made some notes. Then write a letter to Kim accepting the invitation and giving all the necessary information. You must use all your notes.

Guess what? Red Stone are going to be giving a concert at the City Stadium on Saturday 21 July. What about us going to see them together? I know you're a great fan of theirs, but I don't really know anything about them.

Yes!

Tell Kim about the band

I can get tickets if I book them this week. The ticket price depends on whether we sit or stand – could you let me know which you would prefer? Why don't we meet outside the City Stadium at 7 p.m.?

Say which and why

No, suggest different time to Kim

You could stay the night at my new flat, as it's bigger than my old one. We could do something together the next day. Is there anything special you'd like to do?

What about …?

Write a **letter** of between **120** and **180** words in an appropriate style.
Do not write any postal addresses.

Part 2

Write an answer to **one** of the questions 2–5 in this part. Write your answer in **120–180** words in an appropriate style.

---

2   Your teacher has asked you for a report on transport in your local area. Mention the main means of transport used, and suggest how transport facilities could be improved.

Write your **report**.

3   You see this notice on your school noticeboard.

> # SPECIAL PEOPLE
>
> * Who is the most important person in your life?
>
> * Why is this person special to you?
>
> Write us an article for the school magazine answering these questions.

Write your **article**.

4   Your teacher has asked you to write a story for the school's English language magazine. The story must **begin** with the following words:

My day started badly, but it got better and better.

Write your **story**.

5   Answer **one** of the following two questions based on your reading of **one** of these set books. Write the letter **(a)** or **(b)** as well as the number **5** in the question box, and the **title** of the book next to the box. Your answer **must** be about one of the books below.

Best Detective Stories of Agatha Christie – Longman Fiction
Round the World in Eighty Days – Jules Verne
A Tale of Two Cities – Charles Dickens
Animal Farm – George Orwell
More Tales from Shakespeare – Charles and Mary Lamb

Either   **(a)**   What was the most unexpected event in the book or short story you have read? Write a **composition** for your teacher describing what happened and explaining why you were surprised.

Or   **(b)**   An international magazine is publishing articles about its readers' favourite books. Write an **article** explaining why the book or collection of short stories you have read is one of your favourite books.

PAPER 3   USE OF ENGLISH (1 hour 15 minutes)

Part 1

For questions **1–15**, read the text below and decide which answer (**A**, **B**, **C** or **D**) best fits each space. There is an example at the beginning (**0**).

Mark your answers **on the separate answer sheet.**

Example:

0   A priceless   **B** rewarding   **C** precious   **D** prized

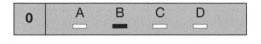

MOUNTAIN CLIMBING

One of the most difficult but **(0)** ..... of pastimes is the sport of mountain climbing. Mountain climbing can be divided into two categories, rock climbing and ice climbing, and the modern climber must **(1)** ..... many different skills.

Rock climbing **(2)** ..... a combination of gymnastic ability, imagination and observation, but perhaps the most necessary skill is being able to **(3)** ..... out how much weight a particular rock will **(4)** ..... . Mountaineers climb in groups of three or four, each climber at a distance of approximately six metres from the next. Usually one person climbs while the other climbers **(5)** ..... hold of the rope. The most experienced climber goes first and **(6)** ..... the other climbers which **(7)** ..... to go. When the leader has reached a good position, he or she makes the rope secure so that it is **(8)** ..... for the others to follow.

Since much mountain climbing **(9)** ..... place in bad weather, snow skills **(10)** ..... a very important part. Ice axes are used for **(11)** ..... steps into the snow, and for testing the ground. Climbers always tie themselves **(12)** ..... , so that, if the leader does fall, he or she can be held by the others and **(13)** ..... back to safety. The number of dangers **(14)** ..... by climbers is almost endless. Yet perhaps the most difficult part of the sport is the physical effort needed when the air has little oxygen. The **(15)** ..... of oxygen can leave mountaineers continually out of breath.

1 **A** own   **B** hold   **C** control   **D** possess

2 **A** requires   **B** insists   **C** calls   **D** orders

3 **A** work   **B** try   **C** stand   **D** set

4 **A** supply   **B** provide   **C** support   **D** offer

5 **A** keep   **B** stay   **C** continue   **D** maintain

6 **A** indicates   **B** signals   **C** points   **D** shows

7 **A** passage   **B** way   **C** walk   **D** course

8 **A** safe   **B** sure   **C** dependable   **D** reliable

9 **A** gets   **B** takes   **C** occupies   **D** fills

10 **A** act   **B** do   **C** play   **D** make

11 **A** cutting   **B** tearing   **C** breaking   **D** splitting

12 **A** collectively **B** jointly   **C** together   **D** co-operatively

13 **A** given   **B** pulled   **C** put   **D** sent

14 **A** marked   **B** touched   **C** felt   **D** faced

15 **A** need   **B** gap   **C** lack   **D** demand

Part 2

For questions **16–30**, read the text below and think of the word which best fits each space. Use only **one** word in each space. There is an example at the beginning (**0**).

Write your answers **on the separate answer sheet**.

Example: | 0 | *of* |

A NEW CRUISE SHIP

One **(0)** ...*of*.... the biggest passenger ships in history, the *Island Princess*, carries people on cruises around the Caribbean. More than double **(16)** .... weight of the *Titanic* (the large passenger ship which sank in 1912), it was **(17)** .... large to be built in **(18)** .... piece. Instead, forty-eight sections **(19)** .... total were made in different places. The ship was then put together **(20)** .... these sections at a shipbuilding yard in Italy.

The huge weight of the *Island Princess* is partly due to her enormous height, **(21)** .... is an incredible forty-one metres. When compared with the *Titanic*, she is also a much broader ship. As **(22)** .... as length is concerned, there's **(23)** .... a great difference, each ship **(24)** .... over two hundred and fifty metres long.

The *Island Princess* can carry **(25)** .... to 2,600 passengers and has 1,321 cabins, including twenty-five specially designed **(26)** .... use by disabled passengers. There is entertainment on board to suit **(27)** .... age and interest, from dancing to good drama. The *Island Princess* seems very likely to be a popular holiday choice for many years to **(28)** .... , even though most people will **(29)** .... to save up in order to be **(30)** .... to afford the trip.

Part 3

For questions **31–40**, complete the second sentence so that it has a similar meaning to the first sentence, using the word given. **Do not change the word given**. You must use between **two** and **five** words, including the word given.

Here is an example (**0**).

Example:

0 You must do exactly what the manager tells you.

carry

You must .... instructions exactly.

The space can be filled by the words 'carry out the manager's' so you write:

0	*carry out the manager's*

Write **only** the missing words on **the separate answer sheet**.

---

31 As a result of the strong wind last night, several tiles came off the roof.

because

Several tiles came off the roof .... so strong last night.

32 In my opinion, Ali is clearly going to be very successful.

doubt

I .... that Ali is going to be very successful.

33 Simona last wrote to me seven months ago.

heard

I .... Simona for seven months.

34 I don't recommend hiring skis at this shop.

advisable

It's .... skis at this shop.

35   Mike's father started the company that Mike now runs.

set

The company that Mike now runs .... his father.

36   The number of car-owners has risen over the past five years.

rise

Over the past five years, there .... in the number of car-owners.

37   'Don't worry Mum, I can look after myself now I'm sixteen,' said Peter.

care

Peter assured his mother that he could .... now he was sixteen.

38   Naomi said that she would never talk to anyone else about the matter.

discuss

Naomi promised never .... anyone else.

39   'This is the best hotel I've ever stayed in,' my colleague said.

never

'I've .... hotel than this,' my colleague said.

40   There were very few people at the concert last night.

came

Hardly .... the concert last night.

Part 4

For questions **41–55**, read the text below and look carefully at each line. Some of the lines are correct, and some have a word which should not be there.

If a line is correct, put a tick (✓) by the number **on the separate answer sheet**. If a line has a word which should **not** be there, write the word **on the separate answer sheet**. There are two examples at the beginning (**0** and **00**).

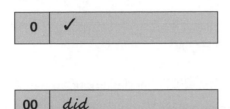

0	✓

Examples:

00	*did*

THE TRAIN JOURNEY

0	You know I was going down to London to stay with my friend
00	Alice during the holidays. Well, the train journey did turned out
41	to be a bit of a disaster! I went to a party the night before I had left,
42	and I woke up quite late enough, so I had to catch the train that
43	left round about midday. At first, I enjoyed the journey as there was
44	another student sitting opposite of me and we started talking.
45	Anyway, when she got out of the train at Oxford, I decided to read
46	my book but, because I hadn't had much sleep on the night before,
47	I soon fell asleep. I must have to slept for over an hour, because
48	I was woke up when all the doors started banging and I realised
49	that everyone was getting out because we were once in London.
50	I jumped up and managed to get myself and my luggage out in
51	a couple of seconds, and breathed a huge sigh of relief. It
52	was only when I had arrived at Alice's house that I have realised I
53	had dropped my address book down when I was getting out of
54	the train. It's a good thing I can properly remember your address,
55	otherwise I wouldn't have been able to write it to you, would I?

Part 5

For questions **56–65**, read the text below. Use the word given in capitals at the end of each line to form a word that fits in the space in the **same** line. There is an example at the beginning (**0**).

Write your answers **on the separate answer sheet**.

Example:	0	*excitement*

PUTTING ON A STAGE SHOW

The opening night of a stage show means (**0**) ...*excitement*... and glamour.	**EXCITE**
Often it also means (**56**) .... problems suddenly arising. And that is even	**EXPECT**
more true if you are planning to take 50 total (**57**) .... and produce the	**STRANGE**
(**58**) .... *South Pacific* in two days. But that's what mother-and-daughter	**MUSIC**
team Linda and Nicki Metz are (**59**) .... offering as a weekend course.	**CURRENT**
The plan seems (**60**) .... , although the two leading parts in the show will be	**AMBITION**
taken by (**61**) .... actors. Technical staff will be on hand to give expert	**PROFESSION**
advice to (**62**) .... Linda says: 'It will be a great weekend for people to do	**PERFORM**
something (**63**) .... and achieve something at the same time. People have	**ENJOY**
a (**64**) .... to work better if they have a deadline. A lot of people also	**TEND**
discover talents that they were (**65**) .... of.'	**AWARE**

PAPER 4   LISTENING (approximately 40 minutes)

Part 1

You will hear people talking in eight different situations. For questions **1–8**, choose the best answer (**A**, **B** or **C**).

---

1   On a train, you overhear a woman phoning her office.
Why has she phoned?

    A   to check the time of an appointment

    B   to apologise for being late

    C   to find out where her diary is

2   You switch on the radio in the middle of a programme.
What kind of programme is it?

    A   a nature programme

    B   a cookery programme

    C   a news programme

3   You overhear a conversation between a watchmaker and a customer.
What does the watchmaker say about the watch?

    A   It is impossible to repair it.

    B   It is not worth repairing.

    C   He does not have the parts to repair it.

4   You overhear a woman talking about her new neighbours.
How does she feel?

    A   offended

    B   shocked

    C   suspicious

5 You hear a man talking about deep-sea diving.
Why does he like the sport?

  A It suits his sociable nature.

  B It contrasts with his normal lifestyle.

  C It fulfils his need for a challenge in life.

6 You turn on the radio and hear a scientist being interviewed about violins.
What is the scientist doing?

  A explaining how a violin works

  B explaining how a violin is made

  C explaining how a violin should be played

7 You hear part of a radio programme about CD ROMs.
What is the speaker's opinion of the CD ROMs about Australia which she tried?

  A Most of them are disappointing.

  B You are better off with an ordinary guidebook.

  C There is little difference between them.

8 You turn on the radio and hear a woman giving advice to business people.
What advice does she give about dealing with customers?

  A Don't let them force you to agree to something.

  B Don't be too sympathetic towards them.

  C Don't allow them to stay on the phone too long.

Part 2

You will hear part of a radio programme in which a woman called Sylvia Short is interviewed about her job. For questions **9–18**, complete the sentences.

Sylvia studied | *and* | **9** | at university.

After university, Sylvia worked as a | **10** | in Italy.

The company which employs Sylvia is called | **11**

Sylvia worked for the company for

| **12** | before becoming the manager's assistant.

Part of Sylvia's job is to organise the

| **13** | in newspapers and magazines.

Sylvia often has to deal with strange questions from | **14**

Sylvia's boss has a radio show on Fridays on the subject of

| **15**

Sylvia has written about her

| **16** | for a new book on Britain.

Sylvia says that in the future she would like to be a

| **17** | on television.

Last year, Sylvia enjoyed attending a | **18** | in Australia.

Part 3

You will hear five different people speaking on the subject of motorbikes. For questions **19–23**, choose the phrase (**A–F**) which best summarises what each speaker is talking about. Use the letters only once. There is one extra letter which you do not need to use.

A the perfect passenger

Speaker 1   **19**

B a feeling of power

Speaker 2   **20**

C a lengthy career

Speaker 3   **21**

D the best way to learn

Speaker 4   **22**

E a family business

Speaker 5   **23**

F a break with routine

Part 4

You will hear part of a radio interview with Steve Thomas, a young chef who has his own cookery series on television. For questions **24–30**, choose the best answer (**A**, **B** or **C**).

---

24 On his TV programme, Steve likes to show audiences

    A   the process of cooking.

    B   amusing incidents.

    C   attractively presented dishes.

	24

25 Steve was given his own TV series because

    A   he cooked for a TV company.

    B   he appeared on a TV programme.

    C   he had been recommended to a TV producer.

	25

26 What made him take up cooking as a child?

    A   His parents expected him to help in their restaurant.

    B   He felt it was the best way of getting some money.

    C   His father wanted to teach him to cook.

	26

27 How did Steve feel once he got to college?

    A   He still found academic work difficult.

    B   He regretted not studying harder at school.

    C   He was confident about his practical work.

	27

28 What does Steve say about the cooks who work for him?

    A   He is sometimes unfair to them.

    B   He demands a lot from them.

    C   He trains them all himself.

	28

29 Steve admires Ron Bell because

    A   he prepares traditional dishes.

    B   he writes excellent articles about food.

    C   he makes a point of using local produce.

	29

30 How will Steve's book be different from other books about cooking?

    A   the varieties of food it deals with

    B   the way that it is illustrated

    C   the sort of person it is aimed at

	30

PAPER 5   SPEAKING (14 minutes)

You take the Speaking test with another candidate, referred to here as your partner. There are two examiners. One will speak to you and your partner and the other will be listening. Both examiners will award marks.

Part 1 (3 minutes)

The examiner asks you and your partner questions about yourselves. You may be asked about things like 'your home town', 'your interests', 'your career plans', etc.

Part 2 (4 minutes)

The examiner gives you two photographs and asks you to talk about them for one minute. The examiner then asks your partner a question about your photographs and your partner responds briefly.

Then the examiner gives your partner two different photographs. Your partner talks about these photographs for one minute. This time the examiner asks you a question about your partner's photographs and you respond briefly.

Part 3 (approximately 3 minutes)

The examiner asks you and your partner to talk together. You may be asked to solve a problem or try to come to a decision about something. For example, you might be asked to decide the best way to use some rooms in a language school. The examiner gives you a picture to help you but does not join in the conversation.

Part 4 (approximately 4 minutes)

The examiner joins in the conversation. You all talk together in a more general way about what has been said in Part 3. The examiner asks you questions but you and your partner are also expected to develop the conversation.

Paper 5 frames

Test 1

Note: In the examination, there will be both an assessor and an interlocutor in the room.
The visual material for **Test 1** appears on pages C1 and C4 (Part 2), and C2–3 (Part 3).

Part 1   (3 minutes / 5 minutes for groups of three)

Interlocutor: Good morning/afternoon/evening. My name is .... and this is my colleague .... He/she is just going to listen to us.
And your names are .... ?
Could I have your mark sheets, please?
Thank you.
First of all we'd like to know something about you, so I'm going to ask you some questions about yourselves.

EITHER (non-UK-based candidates)	*OR (UK-based candidates)*
(Candidate A), do you live in ......? *(name of town where examination is being held)*	Where are you from *(Candidate A)*?
And you *(Candidate B)*?	And you *(Candidate B)*?

- What do you like about living *(here / name of candidate's home town)*?
- And what about you *(Candidate A/B)*?

(Select one or more questions from any of the following categories as appropriate.)

Homelife

- Do you come from a large or a small family? What do you like about living in a *(large/small)* family?
- Does your family live in a house or a flat? Tell me something about it.
- What do you enjoy doing when you're with your family?
- Who are you most similar to in your family? In what ways are you similar?

Work and education

- Do you work or are you a student? Tell me about your day.
- What do you remember most about your early school days?
- Do you think you'll use English in your future work? In what way?
- What sort of job would you like to do in the future? Why?
- Would you like a job in a multinational company? Why?

Personal experiences

- What do you enjoy doing with your friends?
- What's your favourite month of the year? Why?

Leisure time

- What do people do in their free time where you live?
- What do you enjoy doing in the evenings?
- Do you enjoy being on your own? Why?
- Do you often go to the theatre or cinema? What sort of *plays/films* do you like?
- What sports do you enjoy? Do you prefer watching or playing? Why?
- Do you ever play computer games? Why (not)?
- What sort of music do you like?
- Do you prefer live music or listening to recordings? Why?
- Is there any live music in this area? Do you ever go?
- Is your weekend usually relaxing or very busy? Tell me what sort of things you do.
- What did you do last weekend? And what about this weekend, have you got any plans?

The media

- Do you watch TV? What sort of programmes do you like?
- Do you prefer reading newspapers or magazines? What's your favourite *newspaper/magazine*?
- Do you ever use the internet to find out information? What sort of things do you look for?

Travel and holidays

- Do you enjoy travelling? Tell me about a place you've enjoyed visiting.
- Have you ever been on holiday without your family? Where did you go?
- What do you like doing when you're on holiday?
- What was your favourite sort of holiday when you were younger?
- Where would you like to go for your next holiday? Why?

Part 2   (4 minutes / 6 minutes for groups of three)

Interlocutor:	Now, I'd like each of you to talk on your own for about a minute. I'm going to give each of you two different photographs and I'd like you to talk about them. *(Candidate A),* here are your two photographs. They show different places where people work.
	Indicate pictures 1A and 1B on page C1 to Candidate A.
	Please let *(Candidate B)* see them. *(Candidate B),* I'll give you your photographs in a minute. *(Candidate A),* I'd like you to compare and contrast these photographs, and say what you think it is like to work in places like these. Remember, you have only about a minute for this, so don't worry if I interrupt you. All right?
Candidate A:	[*One minute.*]
Interlocutor:	Thank you. [*Retrieve photographs.*] *(Candidate B),* which place would you like to work in?
Candidate B:	[*Approximately twenty seconds.*]
Interlocutor:	Thank you.

Now, *(Candidate B)*, here are your two photographs. They show places that tourists enjoy visiting. Please let *(Candidate A)* have a look at them.

Indicate pictures 1C and 1D on page C4 to Candidate B.

I'd like you to compare and contrast these photographs, and say why you think people choose to go to places like these.
Remember, *(Candidate B)*, you have only about a minute for this, so don't worry if I interrupt you. All right?

Candidate B:	[*One minute.*]
Interlocutor:	Thank you. [*Retrieve photographs.*] *(Candidate A)*, which place would you prefer to visit?
Candidate A:	[*Approximately twenty seconds.*]
Interlocutor:	Thank you.

Part 3 (approximately 3 minutes; 4 minutes for groups of three)

Interlocutor:
Now, I'd like you to talk about something together for about three minutes. I'm just going to listen. *(4 minutes for groups of three.)*
A friend is going to travel around the world for six months. Here are some of the things he might have problems with.

Indicate the set of pictures 1E on pages C2–C3 to the candidates.

First, talk to each other about the problems he might have. Then decide what he could do to avoid these problems.
You have only about three minutes for this. *(4 minutes for groups of three.)*
So, once again, don't worry if I stop you, and please speak so that we can hear you. All right?

Candidates A&B: [*Three minutes.*]

Interlocutor: Thank you.

Part 4 (approximately 4 minutes)

Interlocutor: *Select any of the following questions as appropriate.*

- Have you ever had problems like these on holiday?
- Do you think it's a good idea to go travelling for six months?
- If you could go travelling for six months, who would you take with you? Why?
- What's the most interesting journey you've ever made?
- What advice would you give someone visiting your country for the first time?
- Do you usually listen when people give <u>you</u> advice? Why (not)?

Thank you. That is the end of the test.

Test 2

Note: In the examination, there will be both an assessor and an interlocutor in the room.
   The visual material for **Test 2** appears on pages C5 and C8 (Part 2), and C6–7 (Part 3).

Part 1   (3 minutes / 5 minutes for groups of three)

Interlocutor: Good morning/afternoon/evening. My name is .... and this is my
         colleague .... He/she is just going to listen to us.
         And your names are .... ?
         Could I have your mark sheets, please?
         Thank you.
         First of all we'd like to know something about you, so I'm going to ask you
         some questions about yourselves.

EITHER (non-UK-based candidates)	*OR (UK-based candidates)*
(Candidate A), do you live in ......?	Where are you from *(Candidate A)*?
(name of town where examination is being held)	
And you *(Candidate B)*?	And you *(Candidate B)*?

• What do you like about living *(here / name of candidate's home town)*?
• And what about you, *(Candidate A/B)*?

(Select one or more questions from any of the categories on pages 97–98 as appropriate.)

Part 2   (4 minutes / 6 minutes for groups of three)

Interlocutor: Now, I'd like each of you to talk on your own for about a minute.
         I'm going to give each of you two different photographs and I'd like you to
         talk about them. *(Candidate A),* here are your two photographs. They show
         friends spending time together.

         Indicate pictures 2A and 2B on page C5 to Candidate A.

         Please let *(Candidate B)* see them.
         (Candidate B), I'll give you your photographs in a minute.
         (Candidate A), I'd like you to compare and contrast these photographs, and
         say what you think the people are feeling.
         Remember, you have only about a minute for this, so don't worry if I
         interrupt you. All right?

Candidate A: [*One minute.*]

Interlocutor: Thank you. [*Retrieve photographs.*]
         (Candidate B), where do you usually meet your friends?

Candidate B: [*Approximately twenty seconds.*]

Interlocutor: Thank you.
         Now, *(Candidate B),* here are your two photographs. They show people
         taking photographs. Please let *(Candidate A)* have a look at them.

         Indicate pictures 2C and 2D on page C8 to Candidate B.

I'd like you to compare and contrast these photographs, and say why you think the photographs are being taken.

Remember, *(Candidate B)*, you have only about a minute for this, so don't worry if I interrupt you. All right?

Candidate B:	[*One minute.*]
Interlocutor:	Thank you. [*Retrieve photographs.*] *(Candidate A)*, are you any good at taking photographs?
Candidate A:	[*Approximately twenty seconds.*]
Interlocutor:	Thank you.

Part 3 (approximately 3 minutes; 4 minutes for groups of three)

Interlocutor: Now, I'd like you to talk about something together for about three minutes. I'm just going to listen. *(4 minutes for groups of three.)*

People enjoy doing sports for many different reasons. Here are some pictures of popular sports.

Indicate the set of pictures 2E on pages C6–C7 to the candidates.

First, talk to each other about why people choose to do these different kinds of sports. Then decide which sport would be the most difficult to do well. You have only about three minutes for this. *(4 minutes for groups of three.)* So, once again, don't worry if I stop you, and please speak so that we can hear you. All right?

Candidates A&B: [*Three minutes.*]

Interlocutor: Thank you.

Part 4 (approximately 4 minutes)

Interlocutor: *Select any of the following questions as appropriate.*

- Do you think everyone should do some kind of sport Why (not)?
- Are there many places to do sports in your area? How often do you go there?
- Some people feel there is too much sport on television. Do you agree?
- Do you think sports stars earn too much money? Why (not)?
- What sort of person do you most respect?
- Do you think competition in life is a good thing? Why (not)?

Thank you. That is the end of the test.

Test 3

Note: In the examination, there will be both an assessor and an interlocutor in the room.
   The visual material for **Test 3** appears on pages C9 and C12 (Part 2), and C10–11 (Part 3).

Part 1   (3 minutes / 5 minutes for groups of three)

Interlocutor:	Good morning/afternoon/evening. My name is ………… and this is my colleague ………… . He/she is just going to listen to us.

And your names are ………… ?
Could I have your mark sheets, please?
Thank you.
First of all we'd like to know something about you, so I'm going to ask you some questions about yourselves.

EITHER (non-UK-based candidates)	*OR (UK-based candidates)*
(Candidate A), do you live in ……?	Where are you from *(Candidate A)*?
(name of town where examination is being held)	
And you *(Candidate B)*?	And you *(Candidate B)*?

- What do you like about living *(here / name of candidate's home town)*?
- And what about you *(Candidate A/B)*?

(Select one or more questions from any of the categories on pages 97–98 as appropriate.)

Part 2   (4 minutes / 6 minutes for groups of three)

Interlocutor: Now, I'd like each of you to talk on your own for about a minute.
   I'm going to give each of you two different photographs and I'd like you to talk about them. *(Candidate A),* here are your two photographs. They show people with presents.

Indicate pictures 3A and 3B on page C9 to Candidate A.

Please let *(Candidate B)* see them.
(Candidate B), I'll give you your photographs in a minute.
(Candidate A), I'd like you to compare and contrast these photographs, and say what you think the people are feeling.
Remember, you have only about a minute for this, so don't worry if I interrupt you. All right?

Candidate A: [*One minute.*]

Interlocutor: Thank you. [*Retrieve photographs.*]
   (Candidate B), do you like getting surprises?

Candidate B: [*Approximately twenty seconds.*]

Interlocutor: Thank you.
   Now, *(Candidate B),* here are your two photographs. They show people playing music. Please let *(Candidate A)* have a look at them.

Indicate pictures 3C and 3D on page C12 to Candidate B.

I'd like you to compare and contrast these photographs, and say what you think is enjoyable about music like this.
Remember, *(Candidate B)*, you have only about a minute for this, so don't worry if I interrupt you. All right?

Candidate B: [*One minute.*]

Interlocutor: Thank you. [*Retrieve photographs.*]
                  (Candidate A), what kind of music do you like?

Candidate A: [*Approximately twenty seconds.*]

Interlocutor: Thank you.

Part 3   (approximately 3 minutes; 4 minutes for groups of three)

Interlocutor: Now, I'd like you to talk about something together for about three minutes. I'm just going to listen. *(4 minutes for groups of three.)*
                  I'd like you to imagine that the headmaster of a school has invited some people to come and talk about their jobs. Here are the people who are going to come.

                  Indicate the set of pictures 3E on pages C10–C11 to the candidates.

                  First, talk to each other about what you think is good and bad about these people's jobs. Then decide which three jobs would be most interesting to hear about.
                  You have only about three minutes for this. *(4 minutes for groups of three.)*
                  So, once again, don't worry if I stop you, and please speak so that we can hear you. All right?

Candidates A&B: [*Three minutes.*]

Interlocutor: Thank you.

Part 4   (approximately 4 minutes)

Interlocutor: *Select any of the following questions as appropriate.*

                  • Do you think it's useful for students to hear about people's jobs?
                  • How well do schools prepare young people for work?
                  • How difficult is it for young people to find work in your country?
                  • How important is it to be happy in your job?
                  • How old should you be before you decide which job to do? Why?
                  • What sort of jobs do most people do in your area?

                  Thank you. That is the end of the test.

Test 4

Note: In the examination, there will be both an assessor and an interlocutor in the room.
   The visual material for **Test 4** appears on pages C13 and C16 (Part 2), and C14–15 (Part 3).

Part 1   (3 minutes / 5 minutes for groups of three)

Interlocutor: Good morning/afternoon/evening. My name is .... and this is my
                  colleague .... He/she is just going to listen to us.
                  And your names are .... ?
                  Could I have your mark sheets, please?
                  Thank you.
                  First of all we'd like to know something about you, so I'm going to ask you
                  some questions about yourselves.

EITHER (non-UK-based candidates)   *OR (UK-based candidates)*

(Candidate A), do you live in ......?   Where are you from *(Candidate A)*?
(name of town where examination is being held)
And you *(Candidate B)*?   And you *(Candidate B)*?

- What do you like about living *(here / name of candidate's home town)*?
- And what about you *(Candidate A/B)*?

*(Select one or more questions from any of the following categories on pages 97–98 as
appropriate.)*

Part 2   (4 minutes / 6 minutes for groups of three)

Interlocutor: Now, I'd like each of you to talk on your own for about a minute.
                  I'm going to give each of you two different photographs and I'd like you to
                  talk about them. *(Candidate A)*, here are your two photographs. They show
                  people painting walls.

                  Indicate pictures 4A and 4B on page C13 to Candidate A.

                  Please let *(Candidate B)* see them.
                  (Candidate B), I'll give you your photographs in a minute.
                  (Candidate A), I'd like you to compare and contrast these photographs, and
                  say why you think the people are painting these walls.
                  Remember, you have only about a minute for this, so don't worry if I
                  interrupt you. All right?

Candidate A: [*One minute.*]

Interlocutor: Thank you. [*Retrieve photographs.*]
                  (Candidate B), do people write on walls in your country?

Candidate B: [*Approximately twenty seconds.*]

Interlocutor: Thank you.
                  Now, *(Candidate B)*, here are your two photographs. They show people
                  enjoying the natural world. Please let *(Candidate A)* have a look at
                  them.

Indicate pictures 4C and 4D on page C16 to Candidate B.

I'd like you to compare and contrast these photographs, and say why you think the people have choosen to go to these places.
Remember, *(Candidate B)*, you have only about a minute for this, so don't worry if I interrupt you. All right?

Candidate B:	[*One minute.*]
Interlocutor:	Thank you. [*Retrieve photographs.*] *(Candidate A)*, would you like to spend time in either of these places?
Candidate A:	[*Approximately twenty seconds.*]
Interlocutor:	Thank you.

Part 3 (approximately 3 minutes; 4 minutes for groups of three)

Interlocutor: Now, I'd like you to talk about something together for about three minutes. I'm just going to listen. *(4 minutes for groups of three.)*
Here are some of the things in life which can affect our happiness.

Indicate the set of pictures 4E on pages C14–C15 to the candidates.

First, talk to each other about how important these things are for a happy life. Then decide which two are the most important.
You have only about three minutes for this. *(4 minutes for groups of three.)*
So, once again, don't worry if I stop you, and please speak so that we can hear you. All right?

Candidates A&B: [*Three minutes.*]

Interlocutor: Thank you.

Part 4 (approximately 4 minutes)

Interlocutor: *Select any of the following questions as appropriate.*

- Will the things that are important to you now still be important when you are older? Why (not)?
- What has been the happiest time in your life?
- Do you like stories with happy endings? Why (not)?
- Some people say that an easy life is a happy life. Do you think this is true? Why (not)?
- In what ways do you think people's lives are happier now than fifty years ago?
- What do you think people can do to make the world a happier place?

Thank you. That is the end of the test.

Marks and results

Paper 1   Reading

Two marks are given for each correct answer in **Parts 1, 2** and **3** and one mark is given for each correct answer in **Part 4**. The total score is then weighted to 40 marks for the whole Reading paper.

Paper 2   Writing

A General Impression Mark Scheme is used in conjunction with a Task-specific Mark Scheme, which focuses on criteria specific to each particular task. The General Impression Mark Scheme summarises the content, organisation and cohesion, range of structures and vocabulary, register and format, and target reader indicated in each task.

A summary of the General Impression Mark Scheme is given below. Trained examiners, who are co-ordinated prior to each examination session, work with a more detailed version, which is subject to updating. The FCE General Impression Mark Scheme is interpreted at Council of Europe Level B2.

For a **Band 5** to be awarded, the candidate's writing fully achieves the desired effect on the target reader. All the content points required in the task are included* and expanded appropriately. Ideas are organised effectively, with the use of a variety of linking devices and a wide range of structure and vocabulary. The language is well developed, and any errors that do occur are minimal and perhaps due to ambitious attempts at more complex language. Register and format which is consistently appropriate to the purpose of the task and the audience is used.

For a **Band 4** to be awarded, the candidate's writing achieves the desired effect on the target reader. All the content points required in the task are included.* Ideas are clearly organised, with the use of suitable linking devices and a good range of structure and vocabulary. Generally, the language is accurate, and any errors that do occur are mainly attempts at more complex language. Register and format which is, on the whole, appropriate to the purpose of the task and the audience is used.

For a **Band 3** to be awarded, the candidate's writing, on the whole, achieves the desired effect on the target reader. All the content points required in the task are included.* Ideas are organised adequately, with the use of simple linking devices and an adequate range of structure and vocabulary. A number of errors may be present, but they do not impede communication. A reasonable, if not always successful, attempt is made at register and format which is appropriate to the purpose of the task and the audience.

For a **Band 2** to be awarded, the candidate's writing does not clearly communicate the message to the target reader. Some content points required in the task are inadequately covered or omitted, and/or there is some irrelevant material. Ideas are inadequately organised, linking devices are rarely used, and the range of structure and vocabulary is limited. Errors distract the reader and may obscure communication at times. Attempts at appropriate register and format are unsuccessful or inconsistent.

For a **Band 1** to be awarded, the candidate's writing has a very negative effect on the target reader. There is notable omission of content points and/or considerable irrelevance, possibly due to misinterpretation of the task. There is a lack of organisation or linking devices, and there is little evidence of language control. The range of structure and vocabulary is narrow and frequent errors obscure communication. There is little or no awareness of appropriate register and format.

For a **Band 0** to be awarded, there is either too little language for assessment (fewer than 50 words) or the candidate's writing is totally irrelevant or totally illegible.

*Candidates who do not address all the content points will be penalised for dealing inadequately with the requirements of the task.

Candidates who fully satisfy the **Band 3** descriptor are likely to demonstrate an adequate performance at FCE level.

Paper 2 sample answers and examiner's comments

The following pieces of writing have been selected from students' answers. The samples relate to tasks in Tests 1–4. Explanatory notes have been added to show how the bands have been arrived at. The comments should be read in conjunction with the task-specific mark schemes included in the keys.

Sample A (Test 1, Question 4 – Composition)

> *Everybody keep saying that being rich and famous is the best thing could happen to them.*
>
> *I don't think so. There are pro and cons on being rich.*
>
> *I think being rich and famous means not having a private life, because everywhere you go you are follow by a photographer. You always have to have a bodyguard for your own safety, and that means never being alone.*
>
> *You always have to be careful of who are you meeting, of what are you wearing.*
>
> *You're allow to be yourself only in your own house.*
>
> *On the other hand, you don't have to worry about not having any money at the end of the month or don't know how to pay the bills.*
>
> *I think the best thing is to have a nice job that you like and earn enough money to allow you to have a nice house with a garden, and some free time to spend with your family and friends.*
>
> *The most important thing in life is being happy and I don't think money makes you happy.*

Comments

Content
Full realisation of the task. Topic well argued.

Accuracy
Mostly minor errors, particularly at the beginning. Generally fluent. Last two paragraphs faultless. Good use of gerunds.

Range
Wide range of structure and vocabulary within the task set.

Organisation and cohesion
Well organised.

Appropriacy of register and format
Consistently appropriate.

Target reader
Would be fully informed.

Band: 5

Sample B (Test 2, Question 5(b) – Article)

> *George Orwell has written real life story about behavior. He described animal live in the farm. But when you read this, you see people in goverment. I never thought that they can behave like creatures. In the beging they are nice and polite for you, they promise everything before you give vote for them. Like policians just to get chair, function. Then they show who they are.*
>
> *I've read this book once in 3 hours, is better then movie. In last part main characters it's mean pig's show us the worse kind of human behave, although the are only animals.*
>
> *I admit that we live in twenty-one centaury and now people are more civilate, for public they give better performance then before. However we had two world war, not very long ago. We are still in dangerous this book is show us that we need still aware of people in goverments.*
>
> *Style of book is informal, book was written in last decade when if someone write about humans, he can't public his story.*
>
> *He reached his target, he wrote about animals to show people behavior very clearly.*

Comments

Content
Considerable irrelevance.

Accuracy
Frequent errors which obscure communication.

Range
Some range attempted.

Organisation and cohesion
Poor organisation.

Appropriacy of register and format
Appropriate.

Target reader
Very negative effect on the target reader.

Band: 1

Sample C (Test 3, Question 1 – Letter)

Dear Sam,

I am very hopefull for you letter. I send you this letter in order to answer in your questions.

First of all I want to tell you that the way of my house was to long over 3 hours because it happened an accident. That accident cause the long traffic jam which I met. On the other hand the weather was very nice with windy and without sunny.

Secondly about the photos, I like them all but I prefer this photo in the sea wich we were together.

Now about the watch. I found it in you bedroom under of your bed. It probably fallen of your hand and went under of you bed. Do you want to send your watch now or when I will come there in September?

Lastly I prefer the countryside because of clean air without pollution. I love the animals, and I hate the cars.

I am looking forward to hearing for you.

love

Comments

Content
All points referred to, but not adequately covered.

Accuracy
Errors distract the reader and obscure communication at times.

Range
Limited range of structure and vocabulary.

Organisation and cohesion
Ideas adequately organised.

Appropriacy of register and format
Appropriate.

Target reader
Message not clearly communicated because of lack of language control.

Band: 2

Sample D (Test 3, Question 3 – Article)

BE SOMEONE FAMOUS FOR A DAY

Nowadays being famous is something difficult but succesful. Although, have you ever though about being famous for just one day?

Now you are given the chance. If I had to choose between the most famous people in the world I would probably choose Celine Dyon. The reason why I prefer her is that she is quite rich, succesful and happy with her husband.

Furthermore, I believe that no matter how rich she is, she is also magnificent and beautiful which is also very important. That always give to a woman the chance to be spectacular and wanted by everyone.

In addition she has succeeded in combining both carriere and motherhood which is quite good and important today.

In conclusion I would like to mention that being given the opportunity to make family, be rich, and succesful is what a young woman may want.

Comments

Content
Appropriate coverage of the question.

Accuracy
Reasonably accurate.

Range
Some good vocabulary, but some misuse of individual words, e.g. although, spectacular.

Organisation and cohesion
Good organisation and cohesion.

Appropriacy of register and format
Appropriate.

Target reader
Would be informed.

Band: 3

Sample E (Test 4, Question 2 – Report)

From: Costar Papadopolou

To: Mrs Spyropoulou

Subject: Transport in our area.

As asked, I am writing a report about the transport in our local area, Athens. The report is being handled after a careful examination and deep searching and talking with the citizens of our city.

The main means of transport is the bus and the tube. Thousands of people use these two means of transport to commute, every day. Another popular means of transport is the troley. Taxi, is a very popular means of transport too, although it is much more expensive than the public means of transport mentioned above.

In general, people are not satisfied with the current transport facilities used, although a huge progress has been made the last decade.

In my opinion, people are quite right. Bus stops are often open to rain and some buses are too old to be used. New buses are required in order to make commuting more convenient. Another thing that must be improved, is the timetabe of all public means of transport.

Comments

Content
Good realisation of task.

Accuracy
Generally accurate.

Range
Good range of structure and vocabulary.

Organisation and cohesion
Good organisation.

Appropriacy of register and format
Appropriate.

Target reader
Positive effect on target reader.

Band: 4

Paper 3 Use of English

One mark is given for each correct answer in **Parts 1, 2, 4** and **5**. For **Part 3**, candidates are awarded a mark of 2, 1 or 0 for each question according to the accuracy of their response. Correct spelling is required in **Parts 2, 3, 4** and **5**. The total mark is subsequently weighted to 40.

Paper 4 Listening

One mark is given for each correct answer. The total is weighted to give a mark out of 40 for the paper. In **Part 2** minor spelling errors are allowed, provided that the candidate's intention is clear.

For security reasons, several versions of the Listening paper are used at each administration of the examination. Before grading, the performance of the candidates in each of the versions is compared and marks adjusted to compensate for any imbalance in levels of difficulty.

Paper 5 Speaking

Candidates are assessed on their own individual performance and not in relation to each other, according to the following four analytical critera: grammar and vocabulary, discourse management, pronunciation and interactive communication. These criteria are interpreted at FCE level. Assessment is based on performance in the whole test and not in particular parts of the test.

Both examiners assess the candidates. The assessor applies detailed, analytical scales, and the interlocutor applies a global achievement scale, which is based on the analytical scales.

FCE typical minimum adequate performance

Although there are some inaccuracies, grammar and vocabulary are sufficiently accurate in dealing with the tasks. The language is mostly coherent, with some extended discourse. Candidates can generally be understood. They are able to maintain the interaction and deal with the tasks without major prompting.

Analytical scales

Grammar and vocabulary

This refers to the accurate and appropriate use of grammatical forms and vocabulary. It also includes the range of both grammatical forms and vocabulary. Performance is also viewed in terms of the overall effectiveness of the language used.

Discourse management

This refers to the coherence, extent and relevance of each candidate's individual contribution. In this scale the candidate's ability to maintain a coherent flow of language is assessed, either within a single utterance or within a string of utterances. Also assessed here is how relevant the contributions are to what has gone before.

Pronunciation

This refers to the candidate's ability to produce comprehensible utterances to fulfil the task requirements. This includes stress, rhythm and intonation as well as individual sounds. Examiners put themselves in the position of non-ESOL specialists and assess the overall impact of the pronunciation and the degree of effort required to understand the candidate.

Interactive communication

This refers to the candidate's ability to use language to achieve meaningful communication. This includes initiating and responding without undue hesitation, the ability to use interactive strategies to maintain or repair communication, and sensitivity to the norms of turn-taking.

Global achievement scale

This refers to the candidate's overall performance throughout the speaking test.

Marks

Marks for each scale are awarded out of five: the assessor's marks are weighted singly and the interlocutor's mark is double-weighted. Marks for the Speaking test are subsequently weighted to produce a final mark out of 40.

Test 1 Key

Paper 1 **Reading** (1 hour 15 minutes)

Part 1

1 F   2 A   3 H   4 E   5 B   6 G   7 D

Part 2

8 B   9 D   10 D   11 D   12 C   13 C   14 B

Part 3

15 C   16 E   17 H   18 A   19 F   20 D   21 G

Part 4

22 D   23 A   24/25 A/D (*in either order*)   26 C   27 A   28 C
29 E   30 B   31 E   32 C   33 A   34 E   35 B

Paper 2 **Writing** (1 hour 30 minutes)

Task-specific mark schemes

Part 1

Question 1

Content
The letter must include all the points in the notes:
1) commenting positively on Bill's chapter
2) giving information about parking in city centre
3) giving information about museum opening times
4) reference to map
5) reference to nightlife.

Range
Language appropriate for giving information and making suggestions.

Organisation and cohesion
Letter format, with early reference to why the person is writing. Clear organisation of points. Suitable opening and closing formulae.

Appropriacy of register and format
Informal letter.

Target reader
Would be informed.

Part 2

Question 2

Content
The story should continue from the prompt sentence.

Range
Past tenses. Vocabulary appropriate to chosen topic of story.

Organisation and cohesion
Could be minimally paragraphed. Story should reach a definite ending, even if that ending is somewhat open-ended, as in many modern short stories.

Appropriacy of register and format
Consistent neutral or informal narrative.

Target reader
Would be able to follow the storyline.

Question 3

Content
Article should give opinion(s) about the choice of housing. Acceptable to discuss one type of housing only.

Range
Language of opinion and explanation.

Organisation and cohesion
Clear development of viewpoint with appropriate paragraphing and linking of ideas.

Appropriacy of register and format
Register could range from informal to formal, but must be consistent throughout.

Target reader
Would be able to understand ideas expressed.

Question 4

Content
Composition could agree or disagree with the proposition, or discuss both sides.

Range
Language of opinion and explanation.

Organisation and cohesion
Clear development of viewpoint with appropriate paragraphing and linking.

Appropriacy of register and format
Neutral composition.

Target reader
Would be able to understand ideas expressed.

Question 5(a)

Content
Composition should describe the event in the book that made the strongest impression on the writer and explain why it had such an effect.

Range
Language of narration, description and explanation.

Organisation and cohesion
Clear development of ideas, with appropriate linking and paragraphing.

Appropriacy of register and format
Neutral composition.

Target reader
Would be informed.

Question 5(b)

Content
Composition should give writer's opinion on the statement with reference to one of the characters in the book or short story read.

Range
Language of narration and explanation.

Organisation and cohesion
Clear development of ideas with appropriate linking and paragraphing.

Appropriacy of register and format
Neutral composition.

Target reader
Would be informed.

Paper 3 Use of English (1 hour 15 minutes)

Part 1

1 C   2 A   3 D   4 B   5 D   6 C   7 A   8 A   9 C
10 B   11 C   12 A   13 B   14 A   15 D

Part 2

16 to   17 had   18 not   19 though   20 who / that   21 the
22 in   23 are   24 from   25 so   26 as   27 every / each   28 no
29 like   30 but

Part 3

31 **warned** us | not to sit   32 find our / the | **way** home   33 did / tried my **best** | not to
34 little / no **difficulty** | (in) passing   35 is **somebody** | whose   36 seems / appears | **as**
if / though   37 make (any / much) | **sense** to   38 was that | it was **necessary**
39 we **could** have | done   40 gave us | a **detailed** description

Part 4

41 since   42 made   43 ✓   44 up   45 with   46 an   47 any
48 that   49 of   50 so   51 some   52 much   53 have   54 will   55 ✓

Part 5

56 dangerous   57 performers   58 living   59 incredibly   60 prove
61 safety   62 tiniest   63 careless   64 unlike   65 repeatedly

Paper 4   Listening (approximately 40 minutes)

Part 1

1 C   2 B   3 B   4 C   5 C   6 B   7 A   8 A

Part 2

9 tunnels   10 space (and) fresh air   11 Wales   12 climbing   13 hat
14 lamp   15 boots   16 all ages   17 special interest   18 competitions

Part 3

19 C   20 D   21 B   22 F   23 A

Part 4

24 NO   25 YES   26 NO   27 YES   28 NO   29 YES   30 NO

Transcript   *First Certificate Listening Test. Test One.*

Hello. I'm going to give you the instructions for this test.
I'll introduce each part of the test and give you time to look at the questions.
At the start of each piece you'll hear this sound:

tone

You'll hear each piece twice.

Remember, while you're listening, write your answers on the question paper. You'll have time at the end of the test to copy your answers onto the separate answer sheet.

There will now be a pause. Please ask any questions now, because you must not speak during the test.

[pause]

Now open your question paper and look at Part One.

[pause]

PART 1   *You'll hear people talking in eight different situations. For questions 1 to 8, choose the best answer, A, B or C.*

Question 1   *One.*
You overhear a young man talking about his first job.
How did he feel in his first job?
A bored
B confused
C enthusiastic

[pause]

tone

Man: I didn't want to go to university, so when I finished school, I went and got a job. My parents said if I was in full-time education, they'd give me an allowance, but if not, I'd have to work. So, I got a job in a big store in the menswear department ... Actually, I think I had to go out and find out what I could do because in school I wasn't particularly brilliant, so, when it came to doing work, I think I had to prove a lot of people wrong. So I really felt like doing it ... even though it was just selling socks in Harridges.

[pause]

tone

[The recording is repeated.]

[pause]

Question 2   *Two.*
You hear a radio announcement about a dance company.
What are listeners being invited to?
A a show
B a talk
C a party

[pause]

tone

Man: The Hilton Dance Company have been at the Camden Theatre for almost a month now, offering us a wonderful programme of mainly modern dances. The company have just celebrated their twentieth year of performances all over the world! But this week they'll be taking a break from dancing, to give us an idea of how a dance company works. Top dancer and company manager Lisa West will be in the theatre telling us about the company's work, but all the dancers will be there too, so it's also your opportunity for a get-together! And, of course, you don't need to have any experience of dance for this ...

[pause]

tone

[The recording is repeated.]

[pause]

Question 3

Three.
You overhear a woman talking to a man about something that happened to her.
Who was she?
A a pedestrian
B a driver
C a passenger

[pause]

tone

Woman:	I tell you, we were dead lucky! He could have done some serious damage if we hadn't reacted so quickly.
Man:	What did he do – just shoot straight out without looking?
Woman:	Yeah. Clare yelled something at me and I just slammed on the brakes.
Man:	Did he stop?
Woman:	You're joking! Just blasted his horn at us and carried on.
Man:	And there was nobody behind you?
Woman:	No, fortunately, otherwise who knows what might have happened.
Man:	You were lucky. That road's always busy.

[pause]

tone

[The recording is repeated.]

[pause]

Question 4

Four.
You hear a woman talking on the radio about her work making wildlife films.
What is her main point?
A Being in the right place at the right time is a matter of luck.
B More time is spent planning than actually filming.
C It's worthwhile spending time preparing.

[pause]

tone

Woman: The research for a major wildlife TV series can take up to a year, followed by about two years filming, with four or five camera teams around the world at any one time. Finding the right stories to film is only half the job. The other half is finding the right location and then going out to help the camera-person film it. This can be difficult – you have to make sure you're in the right place at the right time. So good planning is essential. We spend a lot of time on the phone beforehand, getting advice from local experts.

[pause]

tone

[The recording is repeated.]

[pause]

Question 5   *Five.*
You hear part of a travel programme on the radio.
Where is the speaker?
A outside a café
B by the sea
C on a lake

[pause]

tone

Man: This is the most beautiful place I've ever visited and believe me, in my career as a travel writer, I've seen some fabulous scenes. From the deck of this small sailing boat, I have a wonderful view out over a short expanse of sparkling blue water to the white houses of the village on the left, and then to the wooded hillsides behind, which climb up to the snow-covered mountain peaks surrounding this lovely valley. By the water's edge, people are sitting in the late evening sun enjoying a leisurely meal of fresh fish, caught in these waters only a few hours ago. It's heaven!

[pause]

tone

[The recording is repeated.]

[pause]

Question 6   *Six.*
You overhear a woman talking about a table-tennis table in a sports shop.
What does she want the shop assistant to do about her table-tennis table?
A provide her with a new one
B have it put together for her
C give her the money back

[pause]

tone

Woman: Giving me my money back isn't the point. My son needs to practise for an important match, but at the moment his table is lying in bits on the floor. When I bought it, I was assured that it would only take a matter of moments to screw the different parts in place, but the instructions don't make sense. Since I paid so much for it, I think it's only fair to ask for some hands-on help from you in getting it into a usable state. My son is impatient for a game on his new table!

[pause]

tone

[The recording is repeated.]

[pause]

Question 7   *Seven.*
You hear part of an interview with a businesswoman.
What is her business?

A *hiring out boats*
B *hiring out caravans*
C *building boats*

[pause]

tone

Interviewer:	Helen, was this business always a dream of yours?
Woman:	No, not really, it developed from what we used to do, build fishing boats.
Interviewer:	How long have you been in business?
Woman:	About eight years, first we built the marina, then we bought boats to rent out for cruising holidays! It's going well.
Interviewer:	How many boats do you have? During the summer I bet you're pretty busy?
Woman:	Yes, people use them like caravans really, they go up river for their holidays and then bring them back to the moorings here for us to prepare for the next client …

[pause]

tone

[The recording is repeated.]

[pause]

Question 8   *Eight.*
You hear a man talking on the radio.
Who is talking?
A *an actor*
B *a journalist*
C *a theatre-goer*

[pause]

tone

Man:	This is a really delicious part – plenty to get your teeth into, some very good speeches, a lot of change of mood. There's lots for the audience to identify with too, so it all goes to make my job more rewarding. The fact that this is a revival means I also have the challenge of putting my own stamp on a role. The original performance, by the man who created the part some twenty years ago, will still be in the mind of some members of the audience. I couldn't ask for more.

[pause]

tone

[The recording is repeated.]

[pause]

That's the end of Part One.

Now turn to Part Two.

[pause]

PART 2

You'll hear a radio interview with Mike Reynolds, whose hobby is exploring underground places such as caves. For questions 9 to 18, complete the sentences.

You now have forty-five seconds in which to look at Part Two.

[pause]

tone

Interviewer:	In the studio with me today, I have Mike Reynolds who's what is known as a caver. In other words, he spends long periods of time exploring underground caves for pleasure. And Mike's here to tell us all about this fascinating hobby and how to get started on it. So Mike, why caves?
Mike:	Well, cavers actually explore any space that's underground whether it's caves, old mines or tunnels.
Interviewer:	Oh right. So how big are these underground spaces?
Mike:	Oh – anything up to 80 kilometres long … which means that, in some cases, in order to reach the end you've got to sleep, to set up camp, inside the cave at some point – usually where both space and fresh air are available.
Interviewer:	No good if you're afraid of the dark.
Mike:	No.
Interviewer:	So, where do you find the best caves?
Mike:	In terms of countries, the best places are, for example, Ireland, Australia and the Philippines. Here in the UK, various areas have the right sort of geology. My favourite is Wales, but you can find plenty of caves in northern England and in Scotland too.
Interviewer:	Caving involves a lot of physical exercise, doesn't it?
Mike:	That's right … in terms of physical activity, it's very similar to climbing except they go up and we go down. The conditions can be very different though … we often find ourselves facing very small gaps in the rock which we have to crawl through on our hands and knees.
Interviewer:	So the right equipment is obviously very important. If I wanted to start out on a hobby like this, what would I need?
Mike:	Well, you'd need a hard hat, and it's important to get one that fits properly, so that it doesn't keep falling over your eyes or feel too tight, and these can cost anything from five to twenty pounds.
Interviewer:	Umm … that doesn't sound too much for starters.
Mike:	Oh, but then there's the lamp. You wear that on your head because it's very important to keep your hands free at all times. But it doesn't come with the hat and it can cost anything up to fifty pounds to get a suitable one.
Interviewer:	I guess warm clothes are a must too?
Mike:	You'll need to spend thirty to forty pounds on a waterproof suit because the caves can be pretty wet and cold inside and you can get ill if you're not protected. Then, of course, the thing that you really need to spend money on is something for your feet that keeps the water out. Strong boots are essential for this, also because without them you could be slipping on wet surfaces and doing yourself an injury. Cheap ones are just not as safe, I'm afraid.
Interviewer:	It sounds pretty tough. I mean is it really only a sport for the young and fit?
Mike:	That's quite interesting because people tend to think that, but in fact cavers

come from all ages and backgrounds – students and professionals alike. You even find eighty-year-olds who've been doing it for years.

Interviewer: What exactly is it that people find so attractive?

Mike: It's excitement … the pleasure you get in finding something new – a passage that nobody knew about before or a piece of rock that's just lovely to look at.

Interviewer: And I understand that conservation has become a key issue as well?

Mike: Yes. Forty-eight caves in Britain are now known as 'places of special interest' because of what they contain and this is the same in other countries too.

Interviewer: So, do cavers enjoy competing, like in other sports?

Mike: No. We want to enjoy a safe sport and, in order to ensure that, there are no competitions in caving. We try to organise a range of events, but the emphasis is on co-operation and the enjoyment of the sport for what it can offer the individual.

Interviewer: Well, it sounds like something I'll have to try one day. Mike, thank you very much for coming in and sharing …

[pause]

Now you'll hear Part Two again.

tone

[The recording is repeated.]

[pause]

That's the end of Part Two.

Now turn to Part Three.

[pause]

PART 3 *You will hear five different people talking about their work on a cruise ship. For questions 19 to 23, choose from the list, A to F, what each speaker says about their work. Use the letters only once. There is one extra letter which you do not need to use.*

You now have thirty seconds in which to look at Part Three.

[pause]

tone

Speaker 1

[pause]

Man: I deal with anything to do with entertainment on board, and that covers guest lecturers, cabaret artists, the show company and any special nights. I have to plan each cruise with all the performers and then introduce them at the beginning of the show. There's never a dull moment and if I want time to myself, I have to escape to my cabin because a huge part of my job is to mix with people. There are often parties to attend … and then, sometimes, dance nights to organise. So, if I'm not in the shows, I'll be out there dancing with the passengers, because that's part of my job too.

[pause]

Speaker 2

[pause]

Woman: I'm in charge of reception at the Health and Fitness Centre, so I greet passengers and organise their individual fitness programmes and beauty treatments. I wouldn't say it was glamorous because it's very hard work, but the rewards for me are meeting really interesting people, and the system of working. We do eight-month contracts, and once you've finished, it's up to you how much time you have off. Then you renew your contract when you're ready. I like working on a contract basis; I don't like to feel as if I'm stuck somewhere. At home, everyone follows the same nine-to-five pattern. Here, time just has a different meaning.

[pause]

Speaker 3

[pause]

Man: I'm responsible for the safety of the passengers. That means that, apart from keeping an eye on things on a day-to-day basis, I have to make sure that passengers can be safely evacuated if there's an emergency. So, I do a lot of staff training, to make sure each member of staff knows exactly what to do if there's a problem … and, of course, we do emergency drills with the passengers. In theory, I'm on call for twenty-four hours a day, but, in fact, I'm generally on duty for about fifteen so I do get the chance to socialise a bit too. When we're in port, though, I get the whole time off.

[pause]

Speaker 4

[pause]

Woman: There are six photographers here, and we take photos of passengers in various locations on the ship. My main role, though, is to develop and print all the passenger film so I'm less in evidence socially. We don't have set hours because every cruise programme is different and, because I print the photos, I frequently carry on working until six in the morning – getting them ready for the next day. It's quite exciting. People like having their pictures taken with the captain, and we also do quite a few shots in the restaurant and on party nights, but – generally – people come to us with their own requests.

[pause]

Speaker 5

[pause]

Man: I'm in charge of all the restaurants on board. So, menus, costings and the quality of food, plus any staff issues – it's all down to me, I love all that even if the paperwork and accounts can be a bit dull sometimes. But I've worked for this company for nearly 24 years, and I haven't regretted it for one minute. Even though we can't choose where we go, we can put in requests for certain cruises. So, normally, I do four months away and then two months' leave. Where else could you get a job like that and get paid for it? You miss your friends and family, but you don't get time to think about it.

[pause]

Now you'll hear Part Three again.

tone

[The recording is repeated.]

[pause]

That's the end of Part Three.

Now turn to Part Four.

[pause]

PART 4 — *You will hear a radio discussion in which four people are talking about the advertising of children's toys on television. For questions 24 to 30, decide which views are expressed by any of the speakers and which are not. Write YES for those views which are expressed and NO for those which are not expressed.*

You now have forty-five seconds in which to look at Part Four.

[pause]

tone

Interviewer: Today we're talking about the advertising of toys. With me I have Anna Thompson, a member of an environmental group and mother of three, David Wheeler, father of two and manager of a marketing company, and Jim East here is an Advertising Standards Officer who makes the rules about television advertising in Britain. Anna, first, your group has been asking people to stop and think before they go out and buy more toys.

Anna: Yes, parents are under more and more pressure to buy the latest toy for their child and we feel that television advertising is at fault. A lot of it is targeted at children of maybe five or six. There's evidence that these children don't distinguish between the advertisements and the programmes so they enjoy the pictures and the stories and then of course they want the product.

Interviewer: Do you think though that today's children are any different from children ten, twenty, even thirty years ago?

Anna: If you look at the kind of top toys, you'll find that 20, 30 years ago the same toys would run over two, three or four years and now you'll find that there are lots of new ones each year. We're talking about the way new things are pushed at kids, every five minutes practically.

David: Can I just come in there and say that advertising on British television by toy manufacturers to kids is actually decreasing and it has been for the last six years.

Anna: But *spending* on advertising has increased – the advertisements which *do* appear are much more sophisticated and have had more money spent on them.

David:	But for a toy manufacturer to keep its share of the market, it has to do just that. Traditional toys are having a hard time now from all the other things aimed at kids – competition from videos, computer games and the rest. What used to be spent on toys now has to be shared with all these newer and probably more exciting products.
Interviewer:	Jim, what are the rules governing the advertising of toys to children in Britain?
Jim:	OK, very briefly, advertisers are not allowed to say, "go and ask your parents for this product". What they show in terms of the product itself has to reflect what the product can actually do. It mustn't do magical things on television that it can't do in real life.
Interviewer:	I'm a mother of four small children myself and what I wonder when I watch the advertisements is how they can show something which I know is tiny and plasticky but it's shot in such a way – the camerawork and the lighting and stuff – that it looks very attractive. Are they allowed, those sorts of advertisements?
Jim:	Well, in toy advertisements, unlike for other products, advertisers are obliged to show some kind of familiar item that kids will recognise and put it next to the toy so that you can tell how big it really is. Advertisers can, though, show their products in the best light as long as it's not actually misleading.
Interviewer:	How about if toy advertisements weren't allowed until after 8pm, when most children are in bed. What difference would that make? David?
David:	Well, very little, I'd say. For a start 8pm isn't significant: a quarter of all children's viewing takes place after that time, even some of the young children, four to sevens, are watching then. But, really why shouldn't the kids see the adverts?
Anna:	Because advertising is teaching kids that they can use something a few times and then throw it away. It doesn't do them any good and it certainly doesn't do the planet any good.
Jim:	I have to say that we deal with all the complaints about toy advertising on television and we get a handful each year. The research we've done indicates that the majority of people find toy advertising acceptable.
Interviewer:	Well, we have to leave it there, so thank you.

[pause]

Now you'll hear Part Four again.

tone

[The recording is repeated.]

[pause]

That's the end of Part Four.

There'll now be a pause of five minutes for you to copy your answers onto the separate answer sheet.

[Pause the recording here for five minutes. Remind your students when they have one minute left.]

That's the end of the test. Please stop now. Your supervisor will now collect all the question papers and answer sheets.

Goodbye.

Test 2 Key

Paper 1   Reading (1 hour 15 minutes)

Part 1

1 G   2 A   3 D   4 E   5 C   6 F

Part 2

7 C   8 A   9 D   10 A   11 D   12 C   13 D

Part 3

14 C   15 G   16 D   17 F   18 H   19 A   20 E

Part 4

21 B   22 D   23 B   24 F   25 E   26 G   27 F   28 A
29/30 A/G (*in either order*)   31 F   32 E   33 C   34 E   35 C

Paper 2   Writing (1 hour 30 minutes)

Task-specific mark schemes

Part 1

Question 1

Content
Letter must include all the points in the notes:
1) mentioning festival
2) giving information and/or opinion about the hotel
3) suggesting a shop or shops
4) mentioning sports facilities
5) making reference to her offer of a present.

Range
Language appropriate for giving information, making suggestions and thanking.

Organisation and cohesion
Letter format, with early reference to why the person is writing. Clear organisation of points. Suitable opening and closing formulae.

Appropriacy of register and format
Formal letter.

Target reader
Would be informed.

Part 2

Question 2

Content
Article should give information about what type of music the writer would like to hear on the radio and should give at least one suggestion for making the music programme popular.

Range
Language for giving information and making suggestions. Vocabulary relevant to the subject of music and the radio.

Organisation and cohesion
Clear development of article with appropriate paragraphing and linking.

Appropriacy of register and format
Register could range from formal to informal, but must be consistent throughout.

Target reader
Would be informed.

Question 3

Content
Composition should discuss the proposition.

Range
Language of opinion and explanation.

Organisation and cohesion
Clear development of viewpoint with appropriate paragraphing and linking of ideas.

Appropriacy of register and format
Neutral composition.

Target reader
Would be able to understand the writer's point of view.

Question 4

Content
Letter should advise Jo about travelling and working in the writer's country.

Range
Language for giving advice.

Organisation and cohesion
Clear presentation and organisation in the letter. Suitable opening and closing formulae.

Appropriacy of register and format
Informal letter.

Target reader
Would be informed.

Question 5(a)

Content
Composition should discuss the importance of the place(s) and/or people in the book or short story and discuss which is more important.

Range
Language of narration, description and explanation.

Organisation and cohesion
Clear development of ideas, with appropriate linking and paragraphing.

Appropriacy of register and format
Neutral composition.

Target reader
Would be informed about the importance of the place(s) v. people.

Question 5(b)

Content
Article should mention an important day for one of the characters and explain why that day was important.

Range
Language of narration and explanation.

Organisation and cohesion
Clear development with appropriate linking and paragraphing.

Appropriacy of register and format
Register could range from neutral to informal, but must be consistent throughout.

Target reader
Would be informed.

Paper 3 Use of English (1 hour 15 minutes)

Part 1

1 B   2 A   3 A   4 C   5 D   6 A   7 C   8 B   9 C
10 D   11 B   12 C   13 A   14 A⁻   15 B

Part 2

16 all   17 no   18 was   19 used   20 been   21 makes   22 on
23 not   24 good / great   25 yourself   26 take   27 well
28 range / variety / choice   29 for   30 if

Part 3

31 didn't / wouldn't / refused to | **let** Nina   32 **too** complicated | for (any of)
33 not find **any** | shoes which / that   34 didn't | **mean** to   35 made (the / my)
arrangements | for   36 is **said** | to be   37 **prevented** us | (from) enjoying **OR prevented /**

our | enjoying / enjoyment of   38 **seems** to | have left   39 **had** his tooth | taken out / extracted   40 **not** fallen | he would have

Part 4

41 the   42 ✓   43 ✓   44 such   45 too   46 than   47 at
48 more   49 of   50 ✓   51 while   52 in   53 so   54 like   55 to

Part 5

56 mysterious   57 accidentally   58 proof   59 conclusion   60 analysis
61 unlikely   62 scientists   63 doubtful   64 addition   65 truly

Paper 4   Listening (approximately 40 minutes)

Part 1

1 A   2 C   3 B   4 B   5 C   6 A   7 A   8 A

Part 2

9 travel agency   10 High Adventure   11 mending/repairing   12 6 days
13 local   14 bored   15 (enormous) storms   16 (World) Sailing Club
17 (other) ships   18 diaries

Part 3

19 D   20 C   21 F   22 B   23 A

Part 4

24 B   25 C   26 A   27 B   28 B   29 C   30 A

Transcript   *First Certificate Listening Test. Test Two.*

Hello. I'm going to give you the instructions for this test.
I'll introduce each part of the test and give you time to look at the questions.
At the start of each piece you'll hear this sound:

tone

You'll hear each piece twice.

Remember, while you're listening, write your answers on the question paper. You'll have time at the end of the test to copy your answers onto the separate answer sheet.

There will now be a pause. Please ask any questions now, because you must not speak during the test.

[pause]

Now open your question paper and look at Part One.

[pause]

PART 1   *You'll hear people talking in eight different situations. For questions 1 to 8, choose the best answer, A, B or C.*

Question 1   One.
You hear part of an interview in which a film director talks about his favourite movie.
Why does he like the film?
A *It is very funny.*
B *It is very exciting.*
C *It is very romantic.*

[pause]

tone

Interviewer:	So, do you have a favourite movie?
Director:	Oh … that's difficult. Well … I think it has to be *The Agents*, the Mel Rivers movie. I like it because it reminds you that no matter how hard life is, or how many times you get knocked down by bad situations, things can get a whole lot worse.
Interviewer:	When did you first see it?
Director:	On television, late one night … I must have been about 16. There were moments when I just couldn't stop laughing. It's anarchic and silly, but it's very warm. I love the friendship that develops between the two main characters.

[pause]

tone

[The recording is repeated.]

[pause]

Question 2   Two.
You hear a man talking about a sofa he bought.
What's he complaining about?
A *He received the wrong sofa.*
B *The shop overcharged him for the sofa.*
C *The sofa was damaged.*

[pause]

tone

Man:	I think this is the last time I'm buying anything from that shop. I can't believe how inefficient they are! But they've got reasonable prices. The next time I buy a sofa I'd be prepared to pay double to avoid all this stress. They came to deliver it, and when I saw it I thought this isn't the sofa I chose, maybe the colour looks different in daylight. But it was mine. And then I realised that part of the cover at the back was torn and the filling was coming out. So I got them to take it away and now I have to wait two weeks to get it replaced.

[pause]

tone

131

[The recording is repeated.]

[pause]

Question 3

Three.
You hear an actor talking about using different accents in his work.
What point is he making about actors?
A They need to study a wide variety of accents.
B They have to be able to control their use of accents.
C They should try to keep their original accents.

[pause]

tone

Man: Most actors start out with a bit of a regional or non-standard accent of some sort, but what tends to happen is that, at drama school, part of the training is to acquire what's called 'standard English'. So you lose your original accent and when somebody says, you know, 'Do something in your old voice', it takes a couple of minutes to click in and get your head round it again. I phone my parents and they say, 'My, you sound so English', but then over here, I sometimes don't get work because people can hear that I'm actually Australian, so I've got a bit more work to do there.

[pause]

tone

[The recording is repeated.]

[pause]

Question 4

Four.
You hear part of an interview in which a man is talking about winning his first horse race.
What does he say about it?
A He found it rather disappointing.
B He didn't have a chance to celebrate.
C He was too tired to care.

[pause]

tone

Interviewer: Can you still remember the thrill of it? I mean the first time you actually ride out there, out in front must be ...

Man: Yeah, yeah, it was certainly a big thrill, but it was an evening event. It was the last race and it was almost dark by the time we'd finished and when I got home it was about ten or eleven o'clock, so there was very little time to think about it or do anything. And I had to be up at about half five the next day for my job, so unfortunately it was straight back to work really.

[pause]

tone

[The recording is repeated.]

[pause]

Question 5   Five.
              You hear a writer of musicals talking on the radio.
              What's he trying to explain?
              A *why his aunt's career was not very successful*
              B *the difference between American and British musicals*
              C *his reasons for becoming a writer of musicals*

              [pause]

              tone

Man: I was always fascinated by the musical theatre, from the very word go. My aunt was an actress, not a particularly successful one, but I thought her world was unbelievably glamorous. And she used to take me to London to see some of the American musicals which were on in Great Britain some time after they were on in New York, and so I got to see a lot of things at a very early age. It just grabbed me, it was one of those things.

              [pause]

              tone

              [The recording is repeated.]

              [pause]

Question 6   Six.
              You hear the beginning of a lecture about ancient history.
              What's the lecture going to be about?
              A *trade in arms and weapons*
              B *trade in luxury household goods*
              C *trade in works of art*

              [pause]

              tone

Woman: The earliest records of this trade go back to the Ancient Greek period with various deals around the Mediterranean area. Unlike the trade in more decorative or luxury goods, however, few written records remain. So, we mostly rely on archaeological evidence which does show, for example, that designs for swords spread from Greece to the rest of Europe. And using the type of research more usually associated with the spread of artistic trends, we can now show how the equipment necessary to do battle was being exported.

              [pause]

              tone

              [The recording is repeated.]

              [pause]

Question 7 Seven.
You hear a man talking about travelling from London to France for his job.
What does he say about the train journey?
A He's able to use it to his advantage.
B It's a boring but necessary part of his job.
C He enjoys the social aspect of it.

[pause]

tone

Man: The best thing about the Eurostar train is that it is city centre to city centre. I almost always travel with colleagues and we use the train as a second office. Sometimes there are as many as nine of us and I schedule formal meetings to have on the train. I invite suppliers and clients, who have meetings in Paris on the same day, to travel with us so we can discuss business. It's a perfect opportunity to talk without the distractions of the office – we don't switch on our mobile phones.

[pause]

tone

[The recording is repeated.]

[pause]

Question 8 Eight.
You hear a woman in a shop talking about some lost photographs.
What does she think the shop should give her?
A some money
B a replacement film
C an apology

[pause]

tone

Woman: It's no good just standing there saying you're sorry, because that isn't going to give me the photographs you've lost, is it? And I took them on a once-in-a-lifetime holiday, so it's impossible to replace them. It didn't cross my mind for an instant that you could lose a roll of film, just like that. To be frank, I think it's an insult just to offer me a new roll in its place. I would expect at the very least to be offered a refund *and* compensation for the loss and inconvenience, even if it isn't your normal policy.

[pause]

tone

[The recording is repeated.]

[pause]

That's the end of Part One.

Now turn to Part Two.

[pause]

PART 2

You'll hear part of a radio interview with a woman who sailed round the world on her own. For questions 9 to 18, complete the sentences.

You now have forty-five seconds in which to look at Part Two.

[pause]

tone

Interviewer: In the studio this week we have Anna Stephens who returned last July after a non-stop voyage round the world alone. Anna, welcome to the programme. Tell me, how did you get interested in sailing?

Anna: Well, although I was a teacher of sports in a school for a while, it wasn't until I started working for a travel agency that I first went sailing. A colleague invited me and I loved it straightaway. After that I went on several sailing holidays with friends in the Mediterranean.

Interviewer: So, where did you get the idea to sail round the world alone?

Anna: Well, I read a book, 'High Adventure' was the title, which was about a woman sailing alone, and it really impressed me. I suddenly knew what I wanted to do with my life. So I gave up my job and talked a friend into lending me his boat. It was a bit old and rusty, but basically fine. I then spent the next few months mending the boat.

Interviewer: Did you take the boat out to sea to test it?

Anna: Well, that was the problem – I had planned to spend three weeks seeing how the boat performed at sea, but after six days I had to return because it got damaged in bad weather. That was good really because if I'd had three weeks of good weather, I wouldn't have realised what problems I needed to sort out.

Interviewer: What did people say when you had to turn back?

Anna: Oh, some of them thought this proved I wasn't ready for the trip. I would have preferred to carry on with my preparations without telling anybody, but because I relied on money from a number of local companies, they all had to be kept informed of my progress.

Interviewer: Right. Once you finally set out and you were out there alone, did you never feel lonely?

Anna: Well, yes I did, but that wasn't my main problem. The trip was ruined for me by the boat making such slow progress that I got bored. I wanted to be doing something all the time. The only time I really felt busy was in the Southern Ocean, where there were enormous storms and I had plenty to think about all the time.

Interviewer: Were the storms really frightening?

Anna: No, they were the really exciting part. My main difficulty was when I got back home and people didn't believe I'd really done it.

Interviewer: Why did that happen?

Anna: Well, as soon as I returned, I got on the phone to the World Sailing Club to say that I had successfully completed the trip and what did I have to do to get my certificate. They told me to fill in all the forms, etc. Then, on television, people began to say that it was strange although I claimed to have sailed around the world, I had not been in touch with any ships along the way. That's what started it. After that the newspapers were saying I hadn't made the trip at all!

Interviewer: So how did you manage to convince people?

Anna: Well, I showed the sailing club my diaries, which I'd been very careful to keep up-to-date throughout the trip, and they checked them and gave me a certificate. I even got an apology from the newspapers in the end.

Interviewer: And what will your next challenge be?

Anna: I haven't got any firm plans as yet, but I'm writing a book about the trip.

Interviewer: Well, thank you, Anna. We look forward to reading all about it ...

[pause]

Now you'll hear Part Two again.

tone

[The recording is repeated.]

[pause]

That's the end of Part Two.

Now turn to Part Three.

[pause]

PART 3   *You will hear five young people talking about what makes a good teacher. For questions 19 to 23, choose from the list, A to F, which of the opinions each speaker expresses. Use the letters only once. There is one extra letter which you do not need to use.*

You now have thirty seconds in which to look at Part Three.

[pause]

tone

Speaker 1

Girl: Well, I've had lots of teachers who really knew their stuff, I mean, you could ask any question, and you knew you'd get the answer ... But most teachers, when their class was over, that was it, they were gone. You see, a teacher may know a lot, the thing is, it's usually after class that you need their help, often as an individual, if you know what I mean. They think if they just turn up and do the job, that's good enough. I remember one teacher, she was new, said drop in any time. I liked that, I really did ...

[pause]

Speaker 2

Boy: I was always good at maths, and I think it was because I had this excellent teacher, I was lucky really. I didn't like doing my homework, and he'd say, these are the rules, take it or leave it, you do this for tomorrow or you're out of my class. You see, a teacher may be there for you whenever you need his advice, but if he doesn't force you to do your best, it'll all be wasted, won't it?

This teacher had been in the school for many many years, and I know some of the younger teachers didn't like his methods.

[pause]

Speaker 3

Girl: I think it takes some time for a teacher to become really good. Sometimes a teacher who's just starting, well, they can be so demanding, expect a lot, it's as if they want to teach you everything now, if you know what I mean. Some of my friends were always against the teachers who'd been there for a while, and I used to say, well, they're the ones who've gone through all this before, and when they tell me I've done something really well, it means a lot, doesn't it?

[pause]

Speaker 4

Boy: In my opinion, a good teacher has to be able to cover a topic thoroughly. I once had a history teacher who was really kind and helpful, you know, her smile, her manner, like a big sister she was. I was very interested in history at the time, and I realised she didn't exactly ... master the subject ... I think this kind of put me off, although she was always willing to look things up for me in her library, nothing was too much trouble for her. But I sort of lost confidence in her.

[pause]

Speaker 5

Girl: No matter how much a teacher knows about a subject, I think he or she needs to remember that the students are not there to become experts. A good teacher is one that gives encouragement all the time, who tells you when you're making progress, even if it's only very little progress. Of course, a person can know everything about a subject and still be no good as a teacher. We've all had teachers like that, the kind who'll only be satisfied with the highest standards and who will never give you credit for having tried.

[pause]

Now you'll hear Part Three again.

tone

[The recording is repeated.]

[pause]

That's the end of Part Three.

Now turn to Part Four.

[pause]

PART 4

You will hear a radio interview about a mountain-climbing weekend. For questions 24 to 30, choose the best answer, A, B or C.

You now have one minute in which to look at Part Four.

[pause]

tone

Interviewer: My guest today is Douglas Turner, who recently spent a weekend climbing a mountain in Africa. Douglas, how did this come about?

Douglas: Well, I suppose it started with seeing adverts for activity holidays in the national press week after week; it somehow got into my subconscious. Then there was one which said, 'Are you ready for the greatest physical challenge of your life? 5,000 metres. One weekend', and somewhat against my better judgement, I found myself picking up the phone straight away. You see, I simply hadn't trained for it, the nearest I'd got was a bit of hill-walking five years ago.

Interviewer: What did you think you would get out of the weekend?

Douglas: Generally when I go to things I enjoy meeting people, but in this case I was afraid the rest of the group would be a bunch of healthy types, and I wouldn't have much in common with them. And as for the physical effort of climbing the mountain, I thought I'd be lucky if I survived the weekend at all! It was more a kind of wanting to see what I was mentally capable of doing, would I get cold feet and not go at all, or go, but give up halfway up, that sort of thing.

Interviewer: But you made it to the top.

Douglas: Yes, I did. Much to my surprise, I can tell you.

Interviewer: And were you right about the other people?

Douglas: No, actually. There were a few serious walkers and climbers, but most of the participants were professional people who wanted to do something quite different once in a while, more or less like me, in fact. So not intimidating after all. Though I have to admit that nearly all of them were fitter than me. Actually I hadn't realised so many people did this sort of thing. It was funny, when I told a friend that I was going, she said, 'Oh, not another one. Everyone I know's going climbing this year. There's a big thing about pushing yourself to your limit at the moment, isn't there? You're welcome to it,' she said. 'You won't catch me up there.'

Interviewer: How did you all get on together?

Douglas: I suppose we were a bit suspicious of each other at first, but that soon went, and we somehow developed a really close group feeling, and nobody complained about having to wait for the slow ones, which usually included me. Or at least, if they *did* complain, they did it out of earshot. In fact, on the flight home we were busy exchanging cards and decided to book another weekend trip as a party – but without a mountain in sight this time.

Interviewer: So how did the weekend compare with your expectations?

Douglas: It was much better than I'd expected. It made me change, in subtle ways. As I'd hoped, I gained in self-knowledge, and I learnt to get on with people I couldn't escape from, but I also became much more observant, of the tiny little wild flowers, for instance, and that was quite a bonus.

Interviewer: I suppose you're going to be a regular mountain climber now.

Douglas: The pair of boots I wore, I'm keeping with the mud still on them, on my desk at work. They're a kind of trophy, to prove to myself that I've done it. But I somehow don't think I'll be using them again. I'm going to have to put them somewhere less visible, though, because it's sometimes a bit embarrassing when other people are impressed.

Interviewer: Douglas Turner, thank you very much.

Douglas: Thank you.

[pause]

Now you'll hear Part Four again.

tone

[The recording is repeated.]

[pause]

That's the end of Part Four.

There'll now be a pause of five minutes for you to copy your answers onto the separate answer sheet.

[Pause the recording here for five minutes. Remind your students when they have one minute left.]

That's the end of the test. Please stop now. Your supervisor will now collect all the question papers and answer sheets.

Goodbye.

Test 3 Key

Paper 1   Reading (1 hour 15 minutes)

Part 1

1 B   2 F   3 G   4 D   5 E   6 H   7 A

Part 2

8 B   9 C   10 B   11 A   12 B   13 D   14 D

Part 3

15 F   16 B   17 H   18 A   19 D   20 C   21 G

Part 4

22 D   23 B   24 E   25 D   26 A   27 C   28 F   29 A
30 E   31 A   32 C   33 B   34 C   35 C

Paper 2   Writing (1 hour 30 minutes)

Task-specific mark schemes

Part 1

Question 1

Content
Letter must include all the points in the notes:
1) referring to the length of the journey home from the airport
2) describing photo(s)
3) saying where the watch was found
4) mentioning returning the watch
5) referring to what the writer would like to do

Range
Language appropriate for explaining, describing, asking for and giving information.

Organisation and cohesion
Letter format, with early reference to why the person is writing. Clear organisation of points.
Suitable opening and closing formulae.

Appropriacy of register and format
Informal letter.

Target reader
Would be informed.

Part 2

Question 2

Content
Composition could agree or disagree with the proposition, or discuss both sides of the argument.

Range
Language of opinion and explanation.

Organisation and cohesion
Clear development of viewpoint with appropriate paragraphing and linking of ideas.

Appropriacy of register and format
Neutral composition

Target reader
Would be able to understand the writer's point of view.

Question 3

Content
Article should give information about who the writer would choose to be for 24 hours and why. Acceptable for the writer to discuss wider issues relating to the scenario.

Range
Language for giving information and explanation.

Organisation and cohesion
Clear development with appropriate paragraphing and linking.

Appropriacy of register and format
Register could range from informal to formal, but must be consistent throughout.

Target reader
Would be informed.

Question 4

Content
Story should lead up to the prompt sentence.

Range
Vocabulary appropriate for chosen topic for story.

Organisation and cohesion
Could be minimally paragraphed.

Appropriacy of register and format
Consistent neutral or informal narrative.

Target reader
Would be able to follow the storyline.

Question 5(a)

Content
Composition should discuss which character in the book or short story the writer would most like to be.

Range
Language of narration, description and explanation.

Organisation and cohesion
Clear development of ideas, with appropriate linking and paragraphing.

Appropriacy of register and format
Neutral composition.

Target reader
Would be informed.

Question 5(b)

Content
Composition could agree or disagree with the proposition or discuss both sides of the argument with reference to the book or one of the short stories read.

Range
Language of opinion, description, narration and explanation.

Organisation and cohesion
Clear development with appropriate linking and paragraphing.

Appropriacy of register and format
Neutral composition.

Target reader
Would be informed.

Paper 3 Use of English (1 hour 15 minutes)

Part 1

1 B   2 D   3 D   4 A   5 C   6 D   7 A   8 B   9 A
10 C   11 B   12 C   13 A   14 B   15 D

Part 2

16 which / that   17 rid   18 into / to   19 a   20 than   21 before
22 few   23 with   24 of / for   25 all / any   26 not   27 on
28 and   29 so   30 other

Part 3

31 was I put **off** by   32 how I **wide** the / this cupboard   33 **took** George / him ages I to tidy   34 didn't **mean** I to damage   35 **had** her house I designed by
36 **accused** him of I eating   37 had been **paying** I attention   38 was **sorry** I for

having / that she had   **39 could** be difficult / hard | for   **40 ought** to | have asked
(me / permission)

Part 4

41 be   **42** ✓   **43** a   **44** ✓   **45** from   **46** have   **47** would
48 Since   **49** been   **50** ✓   **51** ✓   **52** do   **53** held   **54** to   **55** much

Part 5

56 asleep   **57** energetic   **58** madness   **59** healthy   **60** membership
61 differences   **62** improvement   **63** regularly   **64** harmful   **65** response

Paper 4   Listening (approximately 40 minutes)

Part 1

1 B   2 B   3 C   4 A   5 A   6 C   7 B   8 A

Part 2

9 British Airways / B.A.   10 cabin   11 motorbike   12 Australia
13 helpers   14 fuel   15 9 months   16 sea   17 accurate   18 tired

Part 3

19 D   20 F   21 E   22 A   23 C

Part 4

24 B   25 A   26 C   27 A   28 C   29 B   30 B

Transcript   *First Certificate Listening Test. Test Three.*
Hello. I'm going to give you the instructions for this test.
I'll introduce each part of the test and give you time to look at the questions.
At the start of each piece you'll hear this sound:

tone

You'll hear each piece twice.

Remember, while you're listening, write your answers on the question paper.
You'll have time at the end of the test to copy your answers onto the
separate answer sheet.

There will now be a pause. Please ask any questions now, because you must
not speak during the test.

[pause]

Now open your question paper and look at Part One.

[pause]

PART 1   *You'll hear people talking in eight different situations. For questions 1 to 8, choose the best answer, A, B or C.*

Question 1   One.
               You hear a man talking to a group of people who are going on an expedition into the rainforest.
               What does he advise them against?
               A *sleeping in places where insects are found*
               B *using substances which attract insects*
               C *bathing in areas where insects are common*

               [pause]

               tone

Man: Because you need water for various reasons, you often end up making your overnight camp by a river. Providing you take care to keep insects away, this can be as healthy a place as any. Much as you might feel you need a good wash, one trap not to fall into, though, is the use of soap or shampoo. These may make you feel good, but actually give off unnatural smells in the jungle which act as a magnet to insects, thus increasing the chances of your getting bitten. Better to actually go in for a dip, being careful to dry off and re-apply your anti-insect cream immediately afterwards.

               [pause]

               tone

               [The recording is repeated.]

               [pause]

Question 2   Two.
               You overhear two people talking about a school football competition.
               What did the woman think of the event?
               A *She didn't think anyone had enjoyed it.*
               B *It managed to fulfil its aims.*
               C *Not enough people had helped to set it up.*

               [pause]

               tone

Man: So, how did the school football competition go on Saturday? Sorry I didn't turn up to help, but I had so much to do, you know how it is.
Woman: Oh, don't worry – luckily some of the other parents came along to help. We just didn't attract as many teams as we thought we would, and I thought the whole thing lacked any excitement as a result. You know, of course, that the point was to raise some money to pay for new trees in the school grounds? Well, we achieved that, and my kids thought the whole afternoon was great, so I guess it was OK.

               [pause]

tone

[The recording is repeated.]

[pause]

Question 3
Three.
You hear a woman talking about her studies at the Beijing Opera School.
How did she feel when she first started her classes?
A *worried about being much older than the other students*
B *disappointed because her dictionary was unhelpful*
C *annoyed by the lack of communication with her teacher*

[pause]

tone

Woman: I was twenty-four when I went to China and persuaded the Beijing Opera School to take me on as their first western pupil. I was twice the age of the other students and hardly spoke their language. At the interview I arrived with my little Chinese-English dictionary, which was quite funny as it helped towards persuading them 'cause they thought this girl is so determined. When I actually started the lessons it was very irritating both for me and my teacher. Most of the time we were making signs at each other and misunderstanding. I just had to remain as patient as they were. I learnt the lesson of patience through that school ...

[pause]

tone

[The recording is repeated.]

[pause]

Question 4
Four.
You hear a famous comedian talking on the radio about his early career.
Why is he telling this story?
A *to show how lucky he was at the beginning*
B *to show the value of a good course*
C *to show that he has always been a good comedian*

[pause]

tone

Man: To be honest I sort of fell on my feet. I was doing this course in media studies which meant, you know, looking at cameras and drinking lots of coffee. And one day, we visited a television station as, like, work experience. And they were making this variety show and said they were looking for a new comedian because someone had let them down and so myself and my friend volunteered. It's still a mystery to me why, but they liked us and so I was on live television at the age of about seventeen. We thought we were absolutely brilliant, but I'm glad to say no copy exists of those programmes.

[pause]

tone

[The recording is repeated.]

[pause]

Question 5   *Five.*
                You hear someone talking on the phone.
                Who is she talking to?
                A someone at her office
                B someone at a travel information centre
                C a family member

                [pause]

                tone

Woman: So tell me again, what time does that train get in? I see. That's a bit late,
                because I wouldn't really have enough time to get from the station to my
                meeting. What about the one before that, what time does that one arrive? Yes,
                that sounds better. Is it necessary to book? Will you see to that for me and
                leave the tickets on my desk? No, on second thoughts, I'll be at my mother's
                for the weekend. Can you post them to me there? It'll save time all round.
                Thanks.

                [pause]

                tone

                [The recording is repeated.]

                [pause]

Question 6   *Six.*
                You hear a novelist talking about how she writes.
                How does she get her ideas for her novels?
                A She bases her novels on personal experiences.
                B Ideas come to her once she starts writing.
                C She lets ideas develop gradually in her mind.

                [pause]

                tone

Woman: I get lots of ideas for novels, but I don't necessarily follow them all up. Only
                when they stick around over a period of years do I realise that a particular idea
                has really got a hold on me. That's certainly what happened with my latest
                novel, 'The Red Cord'. Although it's set in my home city of Sydney, Australia,
                the stirrings of an idea came about ten years ago when I was travelling in
                China. This was followed by a long period when the idea occasionally came
                back into my consciousness, each time refined a little more, until I reached a
                point where I thought I'd better start writing.

                [pause]

tone

[The recording is repeated.]

[pause]

Question 7

Seven.
You hear a woman talking to a friend on the phone.
What's she doing?
A *refusing an invitation*
B *denying an accusation*
C *apologising for a mistake*

[pause]

tone

Sue: What do you mean, Mary, when you say, 'I never invite friends round to my house?' No, sorry, I can't accept that. I invited everybody round here for a party on my last birthday, remember? I was going to cook something special for you all and then Henry and Mark insisted on taking us out to that new Japanese restaurant in town. It's true that I accepted their offer, but I thought it would be very rude to refuse.

[pause]

tone

[The recording is repeated.]

[pause]

Question 8

Eight.
You hear a radio announcement about a future programme.
What kind of programme is it?
A *a play about a child*
B *a reading from a children's book*
C *a holiday programme*

[pause]

tone

Man: Memories of long summer days by the sea are recalled in 'The Last Summer', our family drama this afternoon. The Finnish children's writer Tova Janssen, well known for her stories about family life, wrote 'The Last Summer', a magical recreation of her own long childhood summers spent on an isolated island with her grandmother. There are superb performances by Moira Harmer and Alice Williams. Tune in to 'The Last Summer' at two o'clock this afternoon and be transported to an island in a blue sea far away from the world of work.

[pause]

tone

[The recording is repeated.]

[pause]

That's the end of Part One.

Now turn to Part Two.

[pause]

PART 2   *You'll hear an interview with a man who enjoys flying in a small aircraft called a microlight. For questions 9 to 18, complete the sentences.*

You now have forty-five seconds in which to look at Part Two.

[pause]

tone

Interviewer: Now, today I have with me Brian Coleford and he's someone who spends a lot of time up in the air in that smallest of aircraft, the microlight. Hallo Brian.

Brian: Hallo.

Interviewer: But it's more than just a hobby, isn't it?

Brian: Oh yes, I learned to fly when I was at university and I worked as a British Airways pilot for many years until my retirement. These days I spend a lot of my time helping people who want to learn how to fly a microlight, as well as other types of aircraft, at a local flying club.

Interviewer: Tell us about the microlight.

Brian: Well, it's like a very small aircraft, which is powered by an engine. The thing with microlight flying is that it's the closest you can get to actually feeling like a bird because you're out in the open air, there's no cabin or anything around you.

Interviewer: Oh I see …

Brian: And although it's powered, the way it's controlled is by moving your own weight, you steer it by moving your body one way or another.

Interviewer: So you have to lean over like you would on a motorbike?

Brian: You don't lean really, you actually have to push. So you have to be quite fit especially for a long flight.

Interviewer: Which brings us on to the other thing which I know about you and that is that you've recently broken a world record. Tell us about that.

Brian: Well, it involved flying over four continents because I left from London and flew over Europe, Africa and Asia on the way to Australia. No one had ever done that before in a microlight.

Interviewer: The organisation for a long flight must be very difficult indeed, Brian. Surely you didn't do it all on your own?

Brian: Yes, I had no helpers. It was a matter of planning my route in advance and finding out where I'd be able to get fuel en route and knowing how far I could plan to travel safely each day.

Interviewer: So how far can you travel on one tank of fuel?

Brian: Well, I had a special fuel tank fitted – that was the only way in which my microlight was modified for the flight. So that meant I had enough fuel to be able to do about eight hours. The actual distance I covered depended on the winds, of course, but the still-air distance was round about 500 miles a day. It took nine months to plan the 49-day flight, and for each leg I filed a flight plan so that each airport I would land at knew that I was on the way, and if I didn't arrive within half an hour of the time I'd stated, then they'd have started looking for me.

Interviewer: Yes I'm sure that's very necessary. What radio, if any, did you have?

Brian: Yes; I had a two-way VHF radio, but the range of that was only 70 miles, so there was a lot of time when I was out of radio contact with anybody. I crossed thousands of miles of desert and mountain which is quite dangerous, of course, should anything go wrong, and 5,000 miles of the trip was over the sea, which is even more so.

Interviewer: So how did you find your way?

Brian: Well, I had a navigation system which uses satellite signals. It was really easy to use and, I must say, very accurate. I couldn't say I had any problems in knowing where I was or which way I was going.

Interviewer: And what sort of protection did you have? I mean, you weren't just dangling in the cold air, were you?

Brian: Yeah, I just wear a warm flying suit and warm clothes underneath. The coldest was going over the Alps, it was minus 28 degrees there, because I was quite high up. But actually feeling tired was my real problem because it was often dark by the time I landed and I was leaving again at first light. I was never hungry because I was met by such great hospitality everywhere I went. Although sadly I didn't get to see much of the places I visited.

Interviewer: Well, Brian, many congratulations. It's a wonderful achievement and thank you very much for coming in today and talking about …

[pause]

Now you'll hear Part Two again.

tone

[The recording is repeated.]

[pause]

That's the end of Part Two.

Now turn to Part Three.

[pause]

PART 3   *You'll hear five different people talking about short courses they have attended. For questions 19 to 23, choose from the list, A to F, what each speaker says about their course. Use the letters only once. There is one extra letter which you do not need to use.*

You now have thirty seconds in which to look at Part Three.

[pause]

tone

Speaker 1

[pause]

Man: I went on a canoeing course last weekend, rather against my better judgement, because although I enjoy swimming, I thought canoeing might be too difficult. And I was right. I really couldn't get the hang of it. I bet the tutors will remember me: not because I was one of their star students, far from it, but I fell out of the canoe more often than everyone else put together! But even so, I enjoyed it so much that when some of the group signed up to do another course together, in six months' time, I found myself signing up too. I bet the tutors refuse to teach me next time!

[pause]

Speaker 2

[pause]

Woman: It was really good fun: 15 people from all sorts of backgrounds, all desperately trying to speak Italian to each other, and most of us were absolute beginners. We kept falling about laughing, but actually it *did* get a lot easier by the last day, and the tutors were awfully patient. It was held in a big house in the country which now belongs to a university, and the whole thing was brilliant. In fact I don't know how they can do it for what they charged, because it was almost like staying in a luxury hotel. Maybe it was subsidised by the university.

[pause]

Speaker 3

[pause]

Man: It was quite an odd sort of course, in a way, because I expected everyone to be working together, and helping each other to learn, but most of the time we were all just working on our own computers, with the tutor going round and helping each person individually. No teamwork at all. It made me realise that I work much better with other people than on my own: maybe it's poor motivation, or something. Anyway, I learned much more about using a computer, which is what I wanted, so I suppose it was worth it, even though I can't say I enjoyed it much.

[pause]

Speaker 4

[pause]

Woman: I can hardly move, I'm so exhausted. We were out on the courts playing tennis from morning to night, practically. I'm certainly not as fit as I ought to be. I suppose they thought we'd want to play all day to get our money's worth. Well, I could have done with a bit more theory and demonstrations, and a lot more taking it easy! They told me I should go on to the advanced course, next month, but I don't know: I think they have to say that to get the bookings, because they seemed to be saying the same thing to everyone.

[pause]

Speaker 5

[pause]

Man: There were several people I've met on other courses: I haven't been on *that* many, but some of them seemed to take at least a dozen a year. Actually we ended up spending a lot of time chatting and going for walks in the garden, and that kind of made up for the fact that I didn't really learn much about local history, which is why I'd gone. The tutor certainly knew a lot about the subject, but she seemed to have very little idea how to teach, so I just couldn't get into it. And it cost enough. I probably need to find a better way of studying.

[pause]

Now you'll hear Part Three again.

tone

[The recording is repeated.]

[pause]

That's the end of Part Three.

Now turn to Part Four.

[pause]

PART 4 *You will hear part of a radio interview with Martin Middleton, who makes wildlife programmes for television. For questions 24 to 30, choose the best answer, A, B or C.*

You now have one minute in which to look at Part Four.

[pause]

tone

Interviewer: Today's guest needs no introduction. He is a man who has given us hours of interest and entertainment over the years, with his weekly series of wildlife programmes. He is, of course, Martin Middleton. Martin, you've been to the four corners of the Earth in search of material. Where did this love of adventures come from?

Martin: I don't really know … I didn't travel much as a child, but I remember reading about the East and being fascinated by it. Then, when I was about 12, I met someone who'd been to Singapore – and to me that seemed incredible … and, of course, when I started in television, back in the early 1960s, you didn't travel to make a wildlife programme … you went along and filmed at the local zoo. So, when I said I'd like to go and film in Africa, the Head of Programmes just laughed at me.

Interviewer: … and, did you go to Africa?

Martin:	On that occasion, no! But I eventually got them to allow me to go to Borneo in 1962. There was just me and a cameraman. We went off for four months, filming wherever we found something interesting. We bought a canoe, sailed up-river for ten days and ended up in a traditional longhouse. Nowadays, of course, it's all quite different.
Interviewer:	Different? In what way…?
Martin:	We do months of preparation before we set off, so when we start filming, we know exactly what scenes we want to get. I mean, you don't get up in the morning and say to your team, 'What shall we do this morning?' You have to know exactly what each scene is going to show … to work to a strict plan.
Interviewer:	Some of your programmes have taken place in some pretty remote areas. It's hard to imagine other programme-makers wanting to risk the dangers or discomfort that you've experienced.
Martin:	Well, if you want original material – you've got to go off the beaten track … but you can find yourself doing some pretty strange things … um … like, for example, on one occasion, jumping out of a helicopter onto an iceberg. There I was … freezing cold ... then it started to snow … and the helicopter had gone back to the ship and couldn't take off again. So I was stuck there, on this iceberg, thinking, 'This is crazy … I didn't even want to come here!'
Interviewer:	What I wonder is … where does somebody like yourself, who travels to all these exotic places as part of their work, go on holiday?
Martin:	*(laughs)* I'm not very good at lying on a beach – that's for sure. I wouldn't go to a place just to sit around. It's nice to have an objective when you're travelling … to have something you want to film … mm … I've just come back from the Dominican Republic, and we were put up for the first night in a big hotel ... The place was absolutely full of people, just lying there sunbathing. They seemed quite happy to spend the whole day stretched out around the pool … they never seemed to want to go and explore the amazing things there were to see outside the hotel. For me, that would be a very boring way to spend a holiday.
Interviewer:	Your programmes, though, must have inspired a lot of people to take their holidays in remote and little-known places.
Martin:	You are probably right, but …well … I have mixed feelings about all this. I go back to the places where, years ago, I was the only European, and now there are cruise ships coming three times a day. So, you worry that in ten years or so, every remote place on the planet will be swallowed up, because everyone will be visiting it. But, on the other hand, I am in favour of tourism that is done in a way that protects the environment. You can see a good example of this in the Galapagos Islands, where the tourism is carefully managed. That's very successful, and could be a model for the future …

[pause]

Now you'll hear Part Four again.

tone

[The recording is repeated.]

[pause]

That's the end of Part Four.

There'll now be a pause of five minutes for you to copy your answers onto the separate answer sheet.

[Pause the recording here for five minutes. Remind your students when they have one minute left.]

That's the end of the test. Please stop now. Your supervisor will now collect all the question papers and answer sheets.

Goodbye.

Test 4 Key

Paper 1   **Reading** (1 hour 15 minutes)

Part 1

1 B   2 E   3 G   4 D   5 A   6 C   7 F

Part 2

8 D   9 A   10 B   11 D   12 C   13 A   14 D   15 A

Part 3

16 F   17 A   18 D   19 C   20 E   21 H   22 B

Part 4

23 D   24 A   25 B   26 C   27 D   28 A   29 C   30 C
31 B   32 C   33 D   34 A   35 C

Paper 2   **Writing** (1 hour 30 minutes)

Task-specific mark schemes

Part 1

Question 1

Content
Letter must include all the points in the notes:
1) agreeing to go to the concert with Kim
2) giving Kim information about the band
3) explaining whether writer prefers to sit or stand at concert
4) suggesting alternative time to meet
5) suggesting what writer would like to do.

Range
Language appropriate for agreeing, giving information, explaining and suggesting.

Organisation and cohesion
Letter format, with early reference to why the person is writing. Clear organisation of points. Suitable opening and closing formulae.

Appropriacy of register and format
Informal letter.

Target reader
Would have enough information to be able to make the appropriate arrangements.

Part 2

Question 2

Content
Report should state the main means of transport used in the writer's local area and suggest how the transport facilities could be improved.

Range
Language of describing, explaining and suggesting. Also vocabulary appropriate to discussing transport.

Organisation and cohesion
Report should be clearly organised with introduction and conclusion. Sub-headings an advantage.

Appropriacy of register and format
Register could range from neutral to formal but must be consistent throughout. Formal report layout not essential.

Target reader
Would be informed about transport in the writer's area.

Question 3

Content
Article should name an important person in the writer's life and explain why that person is special.

Range
Language of description and explanation.

Organisation and cohesion
Clear development of ideas with appropriate linking and paragraphing.

Appropriacy of register and format
Register could range from informal to neutral but should be consistent throughout.

Target reader
Would be informed about the most important person in the writer's life.

Question 4

Content
Story should continue from the prompt line.

Range
Narrative tenses. Vocabularly appropriate for chosen topic of story.

Organisation and cohesion
Could be minimally paragraphed. Story should reach definite ending, even if that ending is somewhat open-ended, as in many modern short stories.

Appropriacy of register and format
Consistent neutral or informal narrative.

Target reader
Would be able to follow the storyline.

Question 5(a)

Content
Composition should describe the most unexpected event in the book or short story and why the writer was surprised.

Range
Language of description, narration, explanation.

Organisation and cohesion
Clear development of ideas with appropriate linking and paragraphing.

Appropriacy of register and format
Neutral composition.

Target reader
Would be informed.

Question 5(b)

Content
Article should explain why the book or collection of short stories is one of the writer's favourites.

Range
Language of description and explanation.

Organisation and cohesion
Clear development of ideas with appropriate linking and paragraphing.

Appropriacy of register and format
Register could range from neutral to formal but must be consistent throughout.

Target reader
Would be informed.

Paper 3   **Use of English** (1 hour 15 minutes)

Part 1

1 D   2 A   3 A   4 C   5 A   6 D   7 B   8 A   9 B
10 C   11 A   12 C   13 B   14 D   15 C

Part 2

16 the   17 too   18 one   19 in   20 from   21 which   22 far
23 not   24 being   25 up   26 for   27 every / any   28 come
29 have / need   30 able

Part 3

31 **because** the wind | was   32 have / am in | no **doubt**   33 have not **heard** (anything) | from   34 not **advisable** / **advisable** not | to hire (your)   35 was **set** | up by
36 has been | a **rise**   37 take **care** | of himself   38 to **discuss** | the matter with
39 **never** stayed in | a better   40 anybody / anyone | **came** to

Part 4

41 had   42 enough   43 ✓   44 of   45 ✓   46 on   47 to
48 was   49 once   50 ✓   51 ✓   52 have   53 down
54 properly   55 it

Part 5

56 unexpected   57 strangers   58 musical   59 currently   60 ambitious
61 professional   62 performers   63 enjoyable   64 tendency   65 unaware

Paper 4   Listening (approximately 40 minutes)

Part 1

1 A   2 A   3 B   4 C   5 B   6 A   7 A   8 C

Part 2

9 German (and) Spanish   10 (tour) guide   11 World Travel   12 4 months
13 advertising   14 journalists   15 adventure holidays   16 home town
17 presenter   18 conference

Part 3

19 C   20 D   21 F   22 B   23 A

Part 4

24 A   25 B   26 B   27 C   28 B   29 C   30 B

Transcript   *First Certificate Listening Test. Test Four.*
Hello. I'm going to give you the instructions for this test.
I'll introduce each part of the test and give you time to look at the questions.
At the start of each piece you'll hear this sound:

tone

You'll hear each piece twice.

Remember, while you're listening, write your answers on the question paper. You'll have time at the end of the test to copy your answers onto the separate answer sheet.

There will now be a pause. Please ask any questions now, because you must not speak during the test.

[pause]

Now open your question paper and look at Part One.

[pause]

PART 1   *You'll hear people talking in eight different situations. For questions 1 to 8, choose the best answer, A, B or C.*

Question 1   *One.*
On a train, you overhear a woman phoning her office.
Why has she phoned?
A to check the time of an appointment
B to apologise for being late
C to find out where her diary is

[pause]

tone

Woman: Jenny, hi, it's me. I'm on the train and it's stuck somewhere just outside the station – signalling problems or something …Yes, I know, sorry, but there's nothing I can do about it. Anyway, listen, could you check my diary and see when I'm supposed to be with those marketing people … it's on my desk … … Oh, isn't it? Oh, that's strange. And it's not in the drawer? I wonder … Oh, I know, I must have left it in Jimmie's office after yesterday's meeting. You couldn't get it and then ring me back, could you? Sorry to be a nuisance. Thanks a lot.

[pause]

tone

[The recording is repeated.]

[pause]

Question 2   *Two.*
You switch on the radio in the middle of a programme.
What kind of programme is it?
A a nature programme
B a cookery programme
C a news programme

[pause]

tone

Man: Eggs are delicious food and parents have to make sure they are laid in spots well hidden from hungry thieves. One such careful parent braves the rushing waters of the Iguacu Waterfalls in South America to lay its eggs in a damp crack in the rock face behind the falling water. Accidents are frequent, but evidently the risk is considered worthwhile. In any case, there are no eggs on the menu in this particular part of South America, which is bad news for some!

[pause]

tone

[The recording is repeated.]

[pause]

Question 3

Three.
You overhear a conversation between a watchmaker and a customer.
What does the watchmaker say about the watch?
A It's impossible to repair it.
B It's not worth repairing.
C He doesn't have the parts to repair it.

[pause]

tone

Customer: There's something wrong with my watch. It's running slow.
Woman: Oh, a Lexor. It's a common problem with the older Lexor watches. The latest ones are much better!
Customer: That's no help to me.
Woman: No, I suppose not. Anyway, it's not easy to get them fixed, either. Not many people are up to it.
Customer: Right. So ...?
Woman: And the problem is that by the time you've got it to pieces and put in the new parts and reassembled it, you might as well have replaced it. It's always the same, and it's just as likely to go wrong again in a couple of months.

[pause]

tone

[The recording is repeated.]

[pause]

Question 4

Four.
You overhear a woman talking about her new neighbours.
How does she feel?
A offended
B shocked
C suspicious

[pause]

tone

Woman: I must say it surprised me when I saw how many there were in the family. I don't see how they're all going to fit in that small house. And they're obviously quite well-off – you should have seen the amounts of electronic equipment that was carried in, *and* they've got three large cars between them – so why would a wealthy family like that want to live here? It makes you wonder how they earn their living. Not that I've got anything to complain about – they've been perfectly pleasant whenever I've spoken to any of them, though so far they haven't found time to come in for a coffee.

[pause]

tone

[The recording is repeated.]

[pause]

Question 5   *Five.*
You hear a man talking about deep-sea diving.
Why does he like the sport?
A It suits his sociable nature.
B It contrasts with his normal lifestyle.
C It fulfils his need for a challenge in life.

[pause]

tone

Man: I love deep-sea diving. I go at least once every summer. The deeper you go, the quieter everything becomes, until finally all you can hear is the sound of your own heartbeat. It's my way of getting away from it all, finding some peace for once. I spent my honeymoon diving, although my wife's not so keen, and it's not something we always do together. I don't need company necessarily, and I'm not looking for some incredible adventure. I did, however, once join some guys in a cage off Florida, searching for the great white shark. If sharks stop moving, they die. That sounds like me back home.

[pause]

tone

[The recording is repeated.]

[pause]

Question 6   *Six.*
You turn on the radio and hear a scientist being interviewed about violins.
What is the scientist doing?
A explaining how a violin works
B explaining how a violin is made
C explaining how a violin should be played

[pause]

tone

Interviewer: It's difficult to talk about the beauty of a sound, but our great musicians today still clearly feel that these sixteenth-century Italian violins are the best. Do you agree with them?
Scientist: Well, if you look closely at a violin, um … it may be a beautiful-looking instrument, but it is basically just a wooden box, whose function is to take a little energy out of the string that the musician plays and to turn it into sound

that is then heard by the listener. The function of an individual violin is to provide suitable playing and sound qualities for the musician to express all of his or her emotions.

[pause]

tone

[The recording is repeated.]

[pause]

Question 7   *Seven.*
You hear part of a radio programme about CD ROMs.
What is the speaker's opinion of the CD ROMs about Australia which she tried?
A Most of them are disappointing.
B You're better off with an ordinary guidebook.
C There's little difference between them.

[pause]

tone

Woman: If, like me, you're about to set off for Australia and you haven't yet bought a guidebook, how about trying a CD ROM instead? Be careful though, the majority of interactive CDs turn out to be a let down. Many publishers convert printed material to digital format, add a few flashy linkages, and expect the buying public to be impressed. I wasn't. In this context, Wilson's multimedia package is a refreshing contrast. It's got all the information, readily accessed from a single-page pictorial index covering states, cities, wildlife, famous people, etc., and the data is accompanied by good still pictures and 92 video clips.

[pause]

tone

[The recording is repeated.]

[pause]

Question 8   *Eight.*
You turn on the radio and hear a woman giving advice to business people.
What advice does she give about dealing with customers?
A Don't let them force you to agree to something.
B Don't be too sympathetic towards them.
C Don't allow them to stay on the phone too long.

Woman: If you have to deal with a customer who keeps ringing your office about a problem you think you've already dealt with, it's important to be forceful. Make them understand that you really sympathise with their problem, but decide on a course of action early in the conversation and try to keep it moving quickly to avoid any difficult areas. If you can, it might be worth your while trying to discover if there is another reason for their persistence, to try to do something about it before they call again.

[pause]

tone

[The recording is repeated.]

[pause]

That's the end of Part One.

Now turn to Part Two.

[pause]

PART 2   *You will hear part of a radio programme in which a woman called Sylvia Short is interviewed about her job. For questions 9 to 18, complete the sentences.*

You now have forty-five seconds in which to look at Part Two.

[pause]

tone

Interviewer: Good morning, and today we are continuing with our series on careers for young people. In the studio today we have Sylvia Short, who works for a company that produces guidebooks for serious travellers. Now, Sylvia, I believe you left Essex University with a degree in German and Spanish. Tell us something about how you got your job.

Sylvia: My main interest has always been travel. I spent every holiday, when I was a student, travelling abroad. After I left university I spent a year as an English teacher in Spain, followed by six months as a tour guide in Italy. When I returned to England I applied for loads of jobs advertised in the newspaper, but didn't have any success. So I decided to make a list of every company I wanted to work for and write to them directly, rather than wait for them to advertise.

Interviewer: Good advice to anyone, I think.

Sylvia: Yes, and I was very lucky as the company 'World Travel' needed an assistant in their office in London. I dealt mainly with the post at first, just to get used to their way of doing things. Obviously, I was qualified to do more, but I wasn't in a hurry. Then the manager's assistant announced she was leaving after only being with the company for twelve months, and I applied for her job. The company encourages their staff to apply for higher-level jobs and I was promoted four months after joining.

Interviewer: Good for you! What does the job involve?

Sylvia: Well, I've expanded the role since I took it on. I'm in charge of all the advertising in the press whenever we publish a new guidebook and I sometimes give talks to people in the travel industry.

Interviewer: Do you find the work interesting?

Sylvia: Oh, yes, it's never boring. We often get odd requests from journalists. They assume we know everything there is to know about travel so they often ring us to see if we can help them. One rang to say he was writing an article and wanted to know whether there were any female football teams in China.

Interviewer: Really? And what other things do you find yourself doing?

Sylvia:	Oh, a large part of my job is to make sure my boss is where she should be. She does a lot of TV interviews on all aspects of travel and she also presents a radio programme about adventure holidays every Friday night. In between she writes articles and now and again comes into the office to find out what's going on there. My job is to keep her fully informed.
Interviewer:	What do you think you've learnt from working for her?
Sylvia:	Oh, she's an excellent writer and she's helped me, especially when I have to do press releases – she suggests changes, but she's very encouraging, not bossy. She even suggested I did part of a chapter in a new guidebook to Great Britain on my home town, which I enjoyed a lot.
Interviewer:	So, how do you see your career developing?
Sylvia:	Well, I don't think I'm good enough to be a full-time writer. But my boss has a lot of contacts in the TV world, and I fancy becoming a TV presenter. However, at the moment I'm enjoying my job far too much to give it up.
Interviewer:	Do you get to go abroad as part of your job?
Sylvia:	Not as often as you'd think! I do spend a lot of time doing things like answering the phone, but I did manage to go to the company's head office in Australia last year for a conference. That was terrific.
Interviewer:	Sounds to me like you've got the perfect job, Sylvia! Next …

[pause]

Now you'll hear Part Two again.

tone

[The recording is repeated.]

[pause]

That's the end of Part Two.

Now turn to Part Three.

[pause]

PART 3   *You'll hear five different people speaking on the subject of motorbikes. For questions 19 to 23, choose the phrase, A to F, which best summarises what each speaker is talking about. Use the letters only once. There is one extra letter which you do not need to use.*

You now have thirty seconds in which to look at Part Three.

[pause]

tone

Speaker 1

[pause]

Man:	There's nothing like getting on a motorbike, it's wonderful. All my life, I've never travelled any other way. I was eleven years of age when I first started on my brother's bike. I had my licence in 1955 and when a company in Birmingham advertised for a test rider, I applied and got it. I had to ride all the

bikes they made from 1957 through to 1978 which included hill climbs, reliability trials and speedway races. After the company closed down, I did trick riding with my brother. We called ourselves 'The Partners Dare', but by then, of course, it was only a hobby.

[pause]

Speaker 2

[pause]

Man: Well, of course, although many people start off with brothers, fathers or other family members who ride, actually before you go on the road at all in Britain, you've got to take a basic training course and that really gets you off on the right foot. Now, after you've passed that, you're allowed on the road, but we as an organisation strongly recommend that you take further training, and this may be where Dad can help, you know. Then, after that, of course, you're completely free to buy what you like, go on motorways, take passengers and just thoroughly enjoy motorcycling.

[pause]

Speaker 3

[pause]

Woman: I've a passion for my bike because it takes me away from the day-to-day round of family life, as a mother, and the problems of that kind of existence. I can just put the key in, turn it, and I'm in another world. And I can be relieved of all the stresses and strains, just by riding my bike. Then, you may be going along the motorway and if cars are passing you, you do see the women sort of turn and you can lip read them saying 'you look great' or 'well done' and the men always give you a wave in the mirror.

[pause]

Speaker 4

[pause]

Man: The motorbike seems to be an incredibly strong image. This is because it is the perfect form of transport for the individual. You don't have to take account of any other person, you can cut through traffic, on a very simple level, but there's also the idea of the unity of mind, body and machine. It's really the sense of complete freedom, the sense of being completely in control of your own destiny – it's just great fun. You must do it, it's wonderful, you'll enjoy every minute of it.

[pause]

Speaker 5

[pause]

Woman: My mother bought me a bike as soon as I had my licence and she used to ride thousands of miles on the back in those days and then when I started side-car competitions, she used to come with me as the side-car partner. In those days we did a lot of races together – just for fun. She was wonderful, the same weight as me, so the balance was marvellous, and she used to *enjoy* it. I don't know what the rest of the family really thought about it, but my brothers are deeply admiring now, their wives won't let them ride motorbikes, so they look lovingly at mine sometimes.

[pause]

Now you'll hear Part Three again.

tone

[The recording is repeated.]

[pause]

That's the end of Part Three.

Now turn to Part Four.

[pause]

PART 4   *You will hear part of a radio interview with Steve Thomas, a young chef who has his own cookery series on television. For questions 24 to 30, choose the best answer A, B or C.*

You now have one minute in which to look at Part Four.

[pause]

tone

Interviewer: With us today is Steve Thomas, a 23 year-old chef who delights TV audiences with his imaginative cooking programme. Steve, what's the secret of your success?

Steve: Well, I think I'm different from other TV chefs in that I want people to see how I prepare a dish from the word go, so I don't present them with a dish that's half prepared already. If anything should go wrong during the programme, y'know, suppose something gets burned, well, that's part of the experience. When they try preparing it themselves, then they'll see the beauty of the finished product, but not on the screen.

Interviewer: So how did you come to get your own TV series?

Steve: I was working in a restaurant called the Gala in December last year when they came to make a documentary about the place. I didn't even look at the camera. I was too busy making pasta and cooking fish. But the producer spotted me and the following week they phoned me to offer me a job… The Gala owner wished me all the best and let me go without a complaint.

Interviewer: Wow!! Now, is it true that you come from a family of cooks?

Steve: Well, you could say that … I started cooking at the age of eight. My mum and dad have a restaurant and Dad used to do all the cooking back then. My mum was too busy looking after us … Dad insisted that if I wanted some money, I should work for it. And it seemed a lot more interesting to help out in the kitchen and see how things were made than to earn my money washing Dad's car …

Interviewer: You attended a catering course at college. How did you like that?

165

Steve: At school I wasn't very good at anything much. At that time, my mind wasn't on anything other than cooking. I found sitting in a classroom trying to pay attention to things very very trying. I managed to get to college though and there I was fine, because when it came to the actual cooking, I knew what I was doing. I realised that a bit of academic work didn't do you any harm either and I found it much easier when I was interested in the subject, and so I've no regrets, really.

Interviewer: And now you have a TV programme and several cooks working under your orders. How do you get on with them?

Steve: Oh, I love working with them. But on my programme everyone has to be really special. They need to have gone through college training before they even apply for the job. I suppose the problem is that fairly frequently I tend to raise my voice if they don't work efficiently … but I'm just as likely to praise them if they do well … What I say to them is, you want the audience to say we are the best, so we need to make a special effort …

Interviewer: Is there any chef celebrity that you admire especially?

Steve: I definitely think that Ron Bell is the best, and I'm pleased that he's now got his own food column in a newspaper. I had the great privilege of working with him for a while. What's so special about him is that he's always been enthusiastic about using ingredients that come from the area where he works … For example the fish of the day would be the catch from the river close to his restaurant. He's been criticised for sticking to old-fashioned recipes, maybe that's a weakness, but I think that's his decision …

Interviewer: I heard that you are also going to write a book.

Steve: Yes, I'm writing it at the moment. It may disappoint readers who expect a lot of glossy pictures, as most cookbooks nowadays seem to be things to look at rather than read … I've gone for a style that may be less attractive with fewer colour pictures but it will be more useful for most types of reader. What I say in my book is that we must remember the success of a meal does not depend on how it looks … it's what it tastes like and the company of the friends you'll share it with that matters …

Interviewer: Well, thank you, Steve, I look forward to trying some recipes …

[pause]

Now you'll hear Part Four again.

tone

[The recording is repeated.]

[pause]

That's the end of Part Four.

There'll now be a pause of five minutes for you to copy your answers onto the separate answer sheet.

[Pause the recording here for five minutes. Remind your students when they have one minute left.]

That's the end of the test. Please stop now. Your supervisor will now collect all the question papers and answer sheets.

Goodbye.

UNIVERSITY *of* **CAMBRIDGE**
ESOL Examinations

S A M P L E

Candidate Name
If not already printed, write name
in CAPITALS and complete the
Candidate No. grid (in pencil).

Candidate Signature

Examination Title

Centre

Supervisor:
If the candidate is ABSENT or has WITHDRAWN shade here ▭

Centre No.

Candidate No.

**Examination
Details**

0	0	0	0
1	1	1	1
2	2	2	2
3	3	3	3
4	4	4	4
5	5	5	5
6	6	6	6
7	7	7	7
8	8	8	8
9	9	9	9

Candidate Answer Sheet: FCE Paper 1 Reading

Use a pencil

Mark ONE letter for each question.

For example, if you think B is the right answer to the question, mark your answer sheet like this:

0 A B̲ C D E F G H I

Rub out any answer you wish to change with an eraser.

	A B C D E F G H I
1	A B C D E F G H I
2	A B C D E F G H I
3	A B C D E F G H I
4	A B C D E F G H I
5	A B C D E F G H I

	A B C D E F G H I
6	A B C D E F G H I
7	A B C D E F G H I
8	A B C D E F G H I
9	A B C D E F G H I
10	A B C D E F G H I
11	A B C D E F G H I
12	A B C D E F G H I
13	A B C D E F G H I
14	A B C D E F G H I
15	A B C D E F G H I
16	A B C D E F G H I
17	A B C D E F G H I
18	A B C D E F G H I
19	A B C D E F G H I
20	A B C D E F G H I

	A B C D E F G H I
21	A B C D E F G H I
22	A B C D E F G H I
23	A B C D E F G H I
24	A B C D E F G H I
25	A B C D E F G H I
26	A B C D E F G H I
27	A B C D E F G H I
28	A B C D E F G H I
29	A B C D E F G H I
30	A B C D E F G H I
31	A B C D E F G H I
32	A B C D E F G H I
33	A B C D E F G H I
34	A B C D E F G H I
35	A B C D E F G H I

© UCLES 2005 Photocopiable

UNIVERSITY *of* **CAMBRIDGE**
ESOL Examinations

S A M P L E

Candidate Name
If not already printed, write name
in CAPITALS and complete the
Candidate No. grid (in pencil).

Candidate Signature

Examination Title

Centre

Supervisor:
If the candidate is ABSENT or has WITHDRAWN shade here ▭

Centre No.

Candidate No.

**Examination
Details**

0	0	0	0
1	1	1	1
2	2	2	2
3	3	3	3
4	4	4	4
5	5	5	5
6	6	6	6
7	7	7	7
8	8	8	8
9	9	9	9

Candidate Answer Sheet: FCE Paper 3 Use of English

Use a PENCIL (B or HB). Rub out any answer you wish to change with an eraser.

For **Part 1:** Mark ONE letter for each question.
For example, if you think **C** is the right answer to
the question, mark your answer sheet like this:

For **Parts 2, 3, 4** and **5:** Write your answers in
the spaces next to the numbers like this:

0	A B CD

0	*example*

Part 1				
1	A	B	C	D
2	A	B	C	D
3	A	B	C	D
4	A	B	C	D
5	A	B	C	D
6	A	B	C	D
7	A	B	C	D
8	A	B	C	D
9	A	B	C	D
10	A	B	C	D
11	A	B	C	D
12	A	B	C	D
13	A	B	C	D
14	A	B	C	D
15	A	B	C	D

Part 2	Do not write here
16	1 16 0
17	1 17 0
18	1 18 0
19	1 19 0
20	1 20 0
21	1 21 0
22	1 22 0
23	1 23 0
24	1 24 0
25	1 25 0
26	1 26 0
27	1 27 0
28	1 28 0
29	1 29 0
30	1 30 0

**Turn
over
for
Parts
3 - 5
→**

© UCLES 2005 Photocopiable

Part 3 | Do not write here

#		0	1	2
31		31 0	1	2
32		32 0	1	2
33		33 0	1	2
34		34 0	1	2
35		35 0	1	2
36		36 0	1	2
37		37 0	1	2
38		38 0	1	2
39		39 0	1	2
40		40 0	1	2

Part 4 | Do not write here

#		1		0
41		1	41	0
42		1	42	0
43		1	43	0
44		1	44	0
45		1	45	0
46		1	46	0
47		1	47	0
48		1	48	0
49		1	49	0
50		1	50	0
51		1	51	0
52		1	52	0
53		1	53	0
54		1	54	0
55		1	55	0

Part 5 | Do not write here

#		1		0
56		1	56	0
57		1	57	0
58		1	58	0
59		1	59	0
60		1	60	0
61		1	61	0
62		1	62	0
63		1	63	0
64		1	64	0
65		1	65	0

© UCLES 2005 Photocopiable

Activate Learning

UNIVERSITY *of* CAMBRIDGE
ESOL Examinations

S A M P L E

Candidate Name
If not already printed, write name
in CAPITALS and complete the
Candidate No. grid (in pencil).

Candidate Signature

Examination Title

Centre

Supervisor:
If the candidate is ABSENT or has WITHDRAWN shade here

Centre No.

Candidate No.

Examination Details

0	0	0	0
1	1	1	1
2	2	2	2
3	3	3	3
4	4	4	4
5	5	5	5
6	6	6	6
7	7	7	7
8	8	8	8
9	9	9	9

Candidate Answer Sheet: FCE Paper 4 Listening

Mark test version (in PENCIL)

A B C D E

J K

Special arrangements S H

Instructions

Use a PENCIL.
Rub out any answer you
wish to change using an
eraser.

For **Parts 1** and **3:**
Mark ONE letter for each
question.

For example, if you think
B is the right answer to
the question, mark your
answer sheet like this:

0   A   B   C

For **Part 2:**
Write your answer clearly
in the space like this:

0   example

For **Part 4:**
Write ONE letter only.

Part 1

1	A	B	C
2	A	B	C
3	A	B	C
4	A	B	C
5	A	B	C
6	A	B	C
7	A	B	C
8	A	B	C

Part 2

		Do not write here
9		1 9 0
10		1 10 0
11		1 11 0
12		1 12 0
13		1 13 0
14		1 14 0
15		1 15 0
16		1 16 0
17		1 17 0
18		1 18 0

Part 3

19	A	B	C	D	E	F
20	A	B	C	D	E	F
21	A	B	C	D	E	F
22	A	B	C	D	E	F
23	A	B	C	D	E	F

Part 4

		Do not write here
24		1 24 0
25		1 25 0
26		1 26 0
27		1 27 0
28		1 28 0
29		1 29 0
30		1 30 0

© UCLES 2005 Photocopiable

207383